The Coastal Kayaker

D0869476

The Coastal Kayaker

Kayak Camping on
the Alaska and B.C. Coast

by Randel Washburne

Pacific Search Press

Pacific Search Press, 222 Dexter Avenue North, Seattle, Washington 98109
© 1983 by Randel Washburne

Designed by Judy Petry

All photographs, illustrations, and maps are by the author except the following:
   Bill Boehm—pages 132 and 135 (photographs)
   Kevin Cron—pages 111 and 114 (illustrations)

Cover: *Sea lion rookery in Barkley Sound off Vancouver Island (Tom Derrer)*

LIBRARY OF CONGRESS CATALOGING IN PUBLICATION DATA

Washburne, Randel.
      The coastal kayaker.

      Bibliography: p.
      Includes index.
      1. Sea kayaking—Pacific Coast (United States and
Canada) 2. Sea kayaking—Pacific Coast (United States
and Canada)—Guide-books. 3. Camping—Pacific Coast
(United States and Canada) 4. Wilderness areas—Pacific
Coast (United States and Canada)—Description.
5. Pacific Coast (United States and Canada)—Description
and travel—Guide-books. I. Title.
GV776.P3W37   1983   917.9   83-8696
ISBN 0-914718-80-0

Wherever you go and whatever you do in the outdoors, move at Nature's pace, seeking not to impose yourself but to lose yourself. If you must leave footprints, make them not with blindness but with care and awareness of the delicate balance around you. And if you must take souvenirs, take them not in your pockets but in your mind and spirit. In preservation lies the promise of renewal.

Pacific Search Press

Contents

Acknowledgments

For consultation on kayaks and kayaking: Matt Broze, Mariner Kayaks, Seattle; Tom Derrer, Eddyline Kayak Works, Everett; John Dowd, Ecomarine Ocean Kayak Center, Vancouver; Werner Furrer, Everett; Werner A. Furrer, Northwest Design Works, Seattle; Lee Moyer, Pacific Water Sports, Seattle; and Tim Nolan, naval architect, Seattle.

For information on the North Pacific coast, its people, resources, and industries: Embert Demmert, skipper of the seiner *Muzon* and storehouse of knowledge about the Tlingit people; Ed Dillot, Air B.C., Campbell River; Dr. Peter Dooling, Associate Professor, Faculty of Forestry, University of British Columbia; Willie Douglas, Air B.C., Port Hardy; Matthew Fred, Angoon; Mildred Hall, Kenmore Air Harbor, Kenmore; Bonnie Kaden, Alaska Discovery, Gustavus; Dr. Marsha L. Landolt, College of Fisheries, University of Washington; Robert Muth, Regional Social Scientist, U.S. Forest Service, Juneau; Luisa Nishitani, College of Fisheries, University of Washington; and Jeff Osborne, gill-netter *New Hope*.

For photographs and illustrations: Bill Boehm, Tom Derrer, and Kevin Cron.

For editing, word processing, and assistance above and beyond: Linda Daniel, free-lance editor, Seattle; Lorraine Pozzi, Almost Publishing, Seattle; and Toni Reineke, Research Plus, Seattle. To my special friend Linda Daniel I owe particular gratitude. Without her encouragement, ideas, and word-smithery, this book would not have been.

And, finally, for the friendliness and hospitality of the many people who have so enriched my experiences on the North Pacific coast, some in such brief encounters that names were not exchanged. Among them: King Brentzen's tales of mysteries at sea during a stormy night crossing of Queen Charlotte Sound, Eric and Arnold at the pool table in Shearwater, the folks at Tokeen, Ed and Mabel in Rivers Inlet, and the guy on the float-house with the pet crow.

SEA KAYAKS
ON THE
NORTH PACIFIC
COAST

The North Pacific Coast—British Columbia and Southeast Alaska

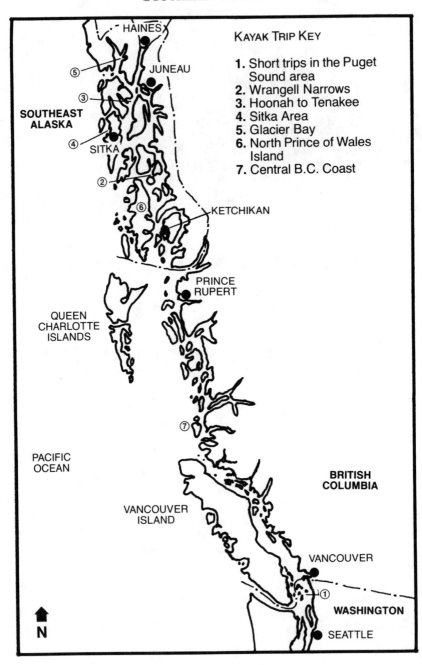

KAYAK TRIP KEY

1. Short trips in the Puget Sound area
2. Wrangell Narrows
3. Hoonah to Tenakee
4. Sitka Area
5. Glacier Bay
6. North Prince of Wales Island
7. Central B.C. Coast

HAINES

JUNEAU

⑤

③

SOUTHEAST ALASKA

④ SITKA

②

⑥ KETCHIKAN

PRINCE RUPERT

QUEEN CHARLOTTE ISLANDS

⑦

PACIFIC OCEAN

BRITISH COLUMBIA

VANCOUVER ISLAND

VANCOUVER

①

WASHINGTON

SEATTLE

N

Welcome to the North Coast

High up on the Pacific coast of North America, the continent spills count-less islands into the sea. Some of them are hundreds of miles in area. Others are but rocks to which a few stricken spruces cling. In return, the ocean probes the mainland repeatedly. Some arms of the sea are seas in their own right, hun-dreds of miles long. Some are incisive fjords. Others are tiny channels, winding to landlocked lagoons they can reach only at high tide. While seeking the North-west Passage in the 1790s, George Vancouver spent three summers exploring these waterways. Yet Vancouver saw but a fraction of them.

From Alaska's Glacier Bay to British Columbia's Vancouver Island is about seven hundred miles as the raven flies. But the convoluted shorelines of the north Pacific archipelago add up to more miles than the circumference of the earth.

Men who lived here centuries ago hewed seaworthy canoes from cedar trunks. Their neighbors to the north developed kayaks of driftwood and skins.

Near Cape Chacon on Prince of Wales Island, Alaska

With these boats, men gained dominion over their world of intertwined land and sea. Today's sea kayaks of plastic resin, Kevlar, or Hypalon are generations removed from their ancestors of cedar and skin. But the labyrinthine wilderness remains. And the kayak is the craft uniquely suited to exploring it.

The pilot waves as he turns his floatplane away from the beach. We stand by our folded kayak and pile of gear as the Beaver roars off down the inlet, spray flying. The engine's pulse echoes from the misted peaks, fading quickly as the plane passes beyond them. We are alone, ten days by paddle from the nearest settlement.

This is wild, remote country. Roads are few. The everyday vehicles are boats and planes. Thus, this coastline is unique in subarctic North America, where development crowds most of the shores. On the north Pacific coast, houses and settlements are rare enough to turn the head of a passerby. Along hundreds of miles of coastline, there is no indication that mankind exists at all. Wildness like this is found elsewhere only in rugged mountains or in inhospitable desert.

It is the wildness that draws people here. They come from all over Canada and the United States. They also come from Britain and New Zealand, the other two great centers of contemporary sea kayaking. The North Coast offers paddlers not only protected waters, a mild summer climate, and spectacular scenery, but also the last of the almost unmanaged wilderness.

Wilderness water travel elsewhere is subtly constrained by the need to protect it from too many enthusiasts. The midwesterner's closest comparable experience is canoe-trekking in Minnesota's huge Boundary Waters Canoe Area. There, reservations are required for paddling a specified route, and still you see other boaters. The north Pacific coast is different because the area is so vast in relation to its recreational use. Water trails are infinite, unmarked, and in their natural state. The managing agencies' presences rarely are felt. In the course of many trips throughout the past ten years, I have only twice encountered United States Forest Service rangers in the wild. I have seen their Canadian counterparts not at all. The result is the feeling that you are the original explorer, discovering just as Captain Vancouver did.

The sea is still. The sky is overcast, but it does not look like rain. This promises to be a good day for traveling toward the low islands lining the horizon to the north. We know little about them other than that the chart shows a maze of tiny channels, some scarcely wide enough for our paddles, and many dry on the low tide. There is one island battered by the open Pacific to the west, but with

Kayak and gear at water's edge on the morning low tide

a small beach on the leeward side. Perhaps we will camp there tonight. Beyond that, who knows?

We assemble our two-seat kayak and set it at the water's edge. Next comes systematic loading of everything into its appointed place: sleeping bags in the bow, food and clothing bags to port and starboard, cooking gear and tent in the stern. The stern seat is mine, with the rudder control at my feet, rain gear at my left knee and charts, cameras, and binoculars at my right.

Easing the laden boat into deeper water, wading in our rubber knee boots on slippery rocks, we attach the rudder, lay paddles across the thwarts, and unzip the spray covers. We are ready to start. I raise a boot from the water, let it drip for a second, then step in. The other foot follows. Settling into the comforting closeness of surrounding duffel, I zip up the cover. The chart goes into its protective bag on the deck in front of me. Pedaling the rudder to seaward with my feet, I dig in with the paddle. A hundred miles of waterways, a thousand islands beckon. And, self-contained, we are on our way.

For many people, enjoyment of wilderness lies in exploring an unknown place, depending on their own judgment and inner resources for meeting its challenges. They want little direction from forest or park management or from

Kayaker follows barges into Wrangell Narrows, Alaska.

guidebook itineraries. They prefer instead to make their own decisions and mistakes, claiming as their own whatever delights or disappointments they find. This book is dedicated to cultivating that sense of independence and discovery.

Planning my own routes and schedules has been a major source of pleasure in trips up north. The journey starts well in advance of departure, as I pore over maps and nautical charts, measure distances over land and sea, locate provisioning points, and read up on things to see along the way. How will I get there? How much time will I need for this trip? What will I need to take with me? What sorts of risks are involved? How much will it cost?

This book will help you plan the kind of trip that will be most enjoyable to you. Emphasis is on proven tools and techniques for going beyond the realm of the guided trip. But I have also suggested itineraries for those who prefer to follow a trail someone else has blazed and enjoyed.

We paddle just offshore in the long evening, which in early summer stretches all the way to midnight. The inlet lies incredibly still. In a grassy clearing ahead by the water's edge we spot our fourth bear of the evening—a big brownie sow. Drifting closer, we see three cubs tumbling at play in the grass.

Paddling softly, hardly breathing, and steering to keep a safe

*margin of water between us and the bears, we drift closer, watching
the youngsters cavort as their mother grazes. Suddenly she rears
upright, revealing her great size. She has caught our scent, but
cannot see us in the twilight. Towering motionless, she tests the air.
The cubs continue to tussle and tumble. Then there is a snort from
Mother—and the clearing is empty.*

Bears, especially the big brownies (known inland as grizzlies), are just one
of the challenges that make the North Coast unique. Paddlers with experience
elsewhere will need some new information and skills in order to get along
safely and comfortably here. For example, everyone knows that it rains. But
there are ways of maintaining a comfortable degree of dryness, warmth, and
cleanliness over a period of weeks in kayak and camp.

Most unusual is the remoteness. This north country demands self-sufficiency. Long-term, total self-containment in the wilderness is something that
only a few of today's kayakers have experienced. Living off the rich resources of
land and sea (where the natives maintained that a man would have to be a fool to
starve to death) is an appealing challenge. But some of the shellfish can kill you.
How do you know which ones are safe?

The ocean here, as elsewhere, has two faces. It can be tranquil almost
beyond belief or awesomely powerful. Sea kayaks and the skills needed to manage them safely are the same worldwide. But here, the remoteness and scarcity
of other boaters puts a heavier burden of judgment on the individual kayaker as
he starts an open-water crossing or negotiates a tidal rapid.

If you are new at sea kayaking, the north Pacific demands that you come
with a basic understanding of your craft and its safe use. I have tried to summarize that critical information for you. And if you are familiar with these con-
cepts, then read on to discover some new points of view on kayak design and
seamanship gathered here.

This book is written for the North Coast resident, too. When it comes to
adapting to the environment, you need no advice from me. But here is a way to
see your own backyard as you probably have not seen it before—by kayak.

*We know there will be Indian ruins in the tiny bay just beyond
the point we're rounding. We rest our paddles and peer ahead as the
little cove drifts into view. Gray, weathered figures stand motionless
along the forest's edge around the crescent beach.*

*Once there was an active village here. Three hundred Haida
built longhouses, crafted canoes, and carved their totems here.
Then, in the 1870s, came smallpox and, soon after, abandonment.
The cedar totems are the century-old legacy, preserved here in what
is now a rarely visited provincial park.*

*A Haida totem in a village abandoned a century ago
in the Queen Charlotte Islands*

Abandoned cannery bunkhouse on a beached barge

Totems and other remnants of human history are the most fragile elements of the North Coast environment. Cabins, canneries, fox farms, mines, and World War II defense installations lie half-hidden in the forest, many remaining much as they were when their occupants left a quarter-century or more ago. These are fascinating to see. And equally impressive is the rate at which the elements are reclaiming the sites. Rainfall fosters rapid and lush growth as well as swift decay.

The biological resiliency of the maritime ecosystem combines with the North Coast's vast size to make it a durable resource. Nature quickly covers our traces. So long as we are careful and responsible in our use of this wild land, kayakers are unlikely to spoil it. Those who come later should be able to enjoy the same full experience—the feeling that we may be at a spot where no one else has been since our grandfathers' time, or may even be at a spot that Grandfather missed.

Paddling into the teeth of a gusting wind, we look in vain for a campsite on the steep, rocky mountainside that rears up from the sea. There is nothing to do but keep going.

Ahead, the chart shows a cannery, but also the ominous legend, "abandoned." Well, at least a cannery site suggests flat ground. Wresting the last mile from the wind and rain, we arrive to find the place a shade short of abandoned. Though the cannery building burned in the 1940s, there remain enough structures to make this a village. Population: two. Gray-haired Ed and Mabel are caretakers. They maintain the docks, warehouses, machine shop, and six cottages for an eventual, but unspecified, return to productivity. They welcome us warmly. Would we like a house in which to stay?

Ed takes us on tour of the tidy, two-bedroom cottages, left over from the days when men fished from skiffs, returning each night to the cannery and their families. But nowadays, throughout the season, a fisherman's boat is his home.

To two wet and weary kayakers, nothing could look more home-sweet-homey than those cottages. Ed switches on the power and lights the oil stove in the one we choose.

We spend the evening with Ed and Mabel, regaled with hot tamales, a town-and-garden tour, and tales of a lifetime on the North Coast. We have only our company to return for their generous hospitality. But here, where visitors are only occasional, that is enough.

Next morning, we're sent on our way with a gift of a dozen fresh eggs, courtesy of the resident flocks of chickens and ducks.

The North Coast attracts special kinds of people. Life "in the bush" is one of the last bastions for the truly independent. Those who choose to make these remote coves and islands their home value individualism, self-sufficiency, privacy, and the sometimes odd ways in which they live. The chance to meet some of these people and to catch a glimpse of the frontier way of life is a special bonus of the North Coast experience.

Most of the bush dwellers welcome a few visitors from time to time. The first kayaker of the season may be greeted as an intrepid adventurer from "Outside." Many respect this person who has come so far in such a little boat, are curious just as the kayaker is, and may invite him or her to share a meal or home. By contrast, the fifth, eighth, or tenth party of a season may strike them understandably as an intrusion to be tolerated, but little more.

If interaction with these people of the North Coast and their unique lifestyles is a high priority for you, travel early in the summer. Steer clear of the well-traveled routes and seek the backwater settlements. There, where ferries do not stop and flights are by charter only, strangers are novelties and kayakers are objects of interest. Stay a day or two, and you will meet everyone in town who has any interest in meeting you.

As the rising tide seeps into the marshland, fingers of barely navigable water creep into the grasses and mud flats ahead. We paddle forward by inches, following the tide and trusting the chart that shows this is the spot where we want to be. We have steered past the false channel that had fooled a paddler we met on the Alaska ferry a few days ago. Over a bit of our brandy, he had described the wrong turn that put him in a dead-end channel instead of at the portage point. But if we are in the right place, where is the other party of kayakers who got off the ferry with us? Our anxiety level rises with the tide. Then we hear their laughter coming from behind. They found the false channel, too.

High tide puts us all one hundred yards from the inlet on the island's other side. We run slings beneath our loaded boats, and with six pairs of hands to lift each one, all kayaks soon are on the other side.

The fellowship (and, at times, the help) of other kayakers can add a lot of enjoyment to a trip. For some people, that kind of companionship outweighs the attractions of adventuring in places more remote. Others want a bit of both.

In this book you will find a section of suggested trips which will serve as guides to kayak touring in places that are easy to reach, attractive to visit, and not far from help and provisions. These are popular trips on which you can expect to see other kayakers. You are likely to find paddlers who have been there before who will offer their advice, and others who plan to follow and will want some advice from you. These trips are not in the wildest country (none pass through country formally designated as wilderness), but they offer scenic, interesting glimpses of off-the-beaten-track places nonetheless. They are intended as satisfying experiences in themselves, and as jumping-off points for kayakers who decide that they are inclined toward further adventuring on their own.

Some of these trips may appeal to people who want to see Southeast Alaska, but find that ferry riding, biking, and/or backpacking give them access to just part of it. Because so much of this area is water, it is difficult to get far from the major towns without a boat. A kayak can be the perfect vehicle for adventuring into the remoteness and viewing the varied life-styles that make Southeast Alaska a special place.

This book will let you know what to expect and how to come equipped for comfort, safety, and fun. It will help you cope with the environment and appreciate the uniqueness of this wilderness whether you choose to paddle along its fringes with fellow travelers or to strike out into it on your own.

Welcome to the North Coast.

Pleasures and Perils

Kayaking on the ocean strikes many people as the ultimate in foolishness. That probably is due to the landsman's perspective of the ocean as foamy combers crashing on the shore. On the other hand, I have encountered the same skepticism from seasoned commercial fishermen. (This makes me wonder, at times, if they know something that I do not! But after ten years of extensive trips along the North Coast, I am still unscathed and paddling.) I think that the experienced seafarer mistrusts kayaks because he does not understand how they are handled when the going gets rough.

A fisherman looks at the outer coastline as a hazard zone, to be avoided at all costs. He knows that out beyond that tumultuous zone lies another world of rolling, but usually harmless, swells. There, a kayak can join larger boats, traveling safely so long as the weather is favorably inclined. But there also is shelter within the turbulent zone, where the larger boats cannot go. There, the kayaker can paddle into the lee of reefs, rocks, and islets, into tranquil coves, sounds, and passages. The north Pacific coastline features all these.

Let us compare the experiences of a kayak and a twenty-two-foot sailboat traveling the same outer coast. There are many offshore rocks and islets as far as a mile out. A moderate wind from seaward helps the sailboat along and creates little resistance for the kayak (except for some annoying chop). The sailors steer carefully offshore of most of the rocks, watching out for entangling kelp beds and feeling uneasy about the onshore wind that could trap them should the engine fail. The kayakers paddle their kayak much closer to shore, picking a winding course through islets, rocks, and kelp, with as much consideration for interesting features as for security.

At one point, the kayakers ride the remainder of a swell through a cleft in a reef just wide enough for the boat. Sea urchins and starfish flash by a few inches below the hull, as the wave carries them over. Ahead, they notice breakers cresting over submerged rocks and adjust their course to pass inshore, where the breakers flatten again to harmless swells.

The wind rises and the choppy seas increase, suggesting that a squall is on the way. The paddlers spot a tiny, protected islet nearby. Hardly a hundred yards wide, it ends in a short beach flanked by Sitka spruce. They decide to haul out and camp. Ten minutes later, the boat is safely stowed in the woods and they are readying diving gear for a raid on the abalone beds.

Meanwhile, the sailors, becoming more uncomfortable by the minute,

Haul-out at day's end

head out to gain sea room and drop their headsail. They, too, have had enough for the day. Starting the engine, they motor along the coast, shipping a faceful of spray with each wave while they search the chart for a secure anchorage. The closest promising-looking one is seven miles away. Realizing that a gale may be developing, they worry about their destination's limited protection from southeasterly winds, and wonder if the bottom there will hold an anchor well. But nothing better presents itself on the chart. So they resign themselves to a rough and worrisome night in a place more than a wet and queasy hour away.

The paddlers are now returning to camp with a bag of abalone. A tent and tarp are pitched where the forest shelters them from wind and rain. This comparative safety and comfort result both from the prudence of the paddlers and the kayak's unsurpassed amphibious ability. By hugging the shore and darting from shelter to shelter along broken coastline, kayakers can keep going in adverse conditions and opt to quit at the slightest excuse for haul-out and shelter. In that, they have much in common with the seals that inhabit this same intertidal zone.

A network of offshore reefs shelters me from the Pacific swells
as I drift, pushed by the breeze. Rounding a point, I spot a harbor

seal hauled out on the rocks just ahead. She's nursing a pup.

Normally, seals bolt for the water when you surprise them. But today, something is different. She shifts uneasily as I approach, but does not fling herself into the sea. Pup nurses on, oblivious to me. I drift closer.

"Take it easy," I say softly, "I'm just passing by." The mother's round, moist eyes hold mine as I drift to within a boat length of her. I am glad I do not have my camera because the obligatory rummaging for it would break the spell.

Pup smacks noisily as he lies on his back, flippers shivering with enjoyment. Mother is relaxed now and, only yards apart, we share a peaceful five minutes.

Slowly I back away and take my leave. Pup never knew of the strange visitor, half man, half boat.

Kayaking affords a degree of intimacy with the coast that is not possible on sailboats, powerboats, or cruise ships. Anchor yourself briefly in a rocky kelp bed, a hoselike strand draped over the boat's bow, and eat a snack while seals rise alongside to gaze. Pull up next to a small iceberg and reach out to feel the deep blue ice, while far away a killer whale blows with gunshotlike reports. The kayaker is an amphibious being, sharing the sea and shoreline with creatures little affected by humans because their impact on the habitat still is a minor one.

Saltwater kayaking has attractions not common to other forms of self-propelled recreation. When backpacking, I often resent being channeled into trails, where every step has been laid out and trod by countless waffle soles before mine, and where every turn may reveal another group of hikers ahead. So, too, with rivers—narrow, one-way corridors where you may have to wait your turn to follow another group through a drop or must win in a lottery to get afloat at all. For kayakers on the north Pacific coast, routes are so unlimited and corridors so wide that chance encounters are unlikely except at a few of the most popular spots.

Another attraction of the sea kayak is its capacity to carry as much as several hundred pounds of cargo without compromising performance or safety. On shorter trips, kayakers can bring bulky canned or fresh foods, even a small ice chest. On one seven-week trip, I carried a ten-band radio, a cassette player, and a tent (with standing headroom and a miniature wood stove). The only real price I paid for traveling heavy was lugging all that gear above the high-tide line each night.

The ocean imposes its moods on the coastal setting more forcefully than inland weather affects mountains, plains, or desert. On two consecutive days, the same inlet can be two different places. A day of battle with churning waves and buffeting headwinds can give way to another of stillness and peace.

Paddling west from Ketchikan, bound for Prince of Wales Island, I am halted by a southeast gale that prevents the long crossing. Morning dawns with the same rain and some fog, but no wind. Eager to be on my way, I decide that I will chance the ten-mile crossing of Clarence Strait. As protection from a possible midchannel capsize and the downpour that will surely seep into my clothes, I don my wet suit. After loading the kayak, I work out a compass bearing that will put me where I want to be on Prince of Wales, invisible in the sea-level clouds and mist that cover the straits.

Setting out, I feel like I am heading into the open Pacific, bound for Japan. I take faith in my chart's assertion that there really is a huge island ahead that I cannot miss. I am reassured by recalling John Dowd's epic hundred-mile passages in open oceans around the world. If he can spend twenty-four hours at sea, surely I can survive three.

Within an hour, my departure point has disappeared astern. My only sense of direction is my compass's small needle, which I keep firmly planted where it should be. The sea remains flat as another hour passes, while the horizon is an unrelieved shading of sea and sky. I pretend I am a seaman on the masthead of an explorer's sailing ship, hoping for a landfall instead of the edge of the earth.

Wedge Island should be a few miles north of me by now. Squinting northward, rejecting mirages, I see something darker. If that is the island, I should soon see the offshore rocks of Prince of Wales's Moira Sound. Ten minutes later, they appear out of the mist. Land ho!

I am almost there, and right where the compass said I should be.

There are risks, of course. Kayakers have drowned in the coastal waters of Alaska and British Columbia. There is no doubt that ocean kayaking carries an element of danger, although I believe it ranks far below that of hang-gliding, rock climbing, and ski mountaineering. It holds fewer inherent hazards than does white-water kayaking.

Most dangerous are the long crossings that sometimes are necessary. Even placid weather can, within an hour, become a violent squall along the north Pacific coast. Hence, crossings more than three miles long are avoided when possible and shorter ones undertaken only when the weather appears to be stable. The wise paddler will turn back rather than struggle against the elements to the point of exhaustion.

Cold ocean water is a killer. For anyone not encased in a wet suit, it is absolutely essential to stay out of the water or to get out within a few minutes.

A killer whale in Icy Strait, Alaska

North Pacific summer water averages between fifty and sixty degrees, temperatures that can bring death from hypothermia in little more than an hour of immersion and incapacitation in far less time.

A proper sea kayak has a low center of gravity. Some have more stability than others, depending on the width and shape of the hull. But protection against upsets in all of them ultimately rests with the balance and paddling skill of the kayaker. An upright boat will not likely fill with spray or waves because spray covers are used to seal the cockpit.

Other hazards include sea lions, which are territorial about the waters around their rookeries and have threatened kayakers. Although there have been no reports of killer whales attacking kayaks, orcas have rammed and sunk small boats elsewhere in the Pacific. Killer whales have passed by me on two occasions, but did not show the slightest interest in me. However, a curious or playful nudge would have been enough to put me in the water. Surfacing whales have been known to dump people out of skiffs, though probably inadvertently. Although such events are unlikely, caution in the presence of larger marine mammals is advised.

Miscellaneous hazards include hull punctures, which sometimes occur when landing or launching and which may be repaired ashore. Running aground is unlikely because a kayak draws little water and shallows are visible or marked by surface disturbances.

In places like South Inian Pass in Cross Sound, near Glacier Bay, there is real danger of being carried out to sea. The ebb tide empties large volumes of water straight out into the Pacific at speeds of up to ten knots. With a maximum paddling speed of four knots, a kayak could be carried a long way from land.

Losing a paddle can bring a quick end to a trip or to a life. A spare or at least a good substitute must be carried.

Dangers that may be encountered ashore include Southeast Alaska's brown bears. They pose a real threat, which causes some kayakers to confine their touring to British Columbia's islands, where only the smaller and less dangerous black bears are found. Camping in bear country takes some special precautions and a bit of fortitude.

Also, out in the wild there is always the possibility of accident or illness. Help may be distant and made more remote by an incapacitated paddler. I still recall the apprehension I felt on my first trip on the Alaska coast. A growing sense of uneasiness gripped me as, day by day, civilization fell astern and four of us paddled deeper into the coastal wilderness. Bears, breakers, injury, sickness.... There is no one to help us out here. What will we do if...?

In a week I grew more comfortable, though still wary. After twenty-eight days, we rounded a point and saw the town that was our final destination. Our jokes about the cold-storage plant being a cookie factory ready to serve us Oreos reflected the lifting of the burden of self-reliance and the interdependence with which we had been tightly bound.

Now, ten years and many North Coast trips later, my foreboding has diminished and my alertness has grown stronger. Sure, I am taking chances in being here and doing this. But experience has given me the ability to anticipate hazards and to do my best to avoid them. I feel more in control, less vulnerable and more able to avoid becoming so. I accept the risks because I, like many others, feel they are a reasonable price to pay for experiences we can savor for the rest of our lives.

The Kayak as
Vehicle and Luggage

With more than thirty kinds of sea kayaks made in the United States and Canada, and another dozen imported from Europe, picking a boat can be as complex as buying a new car. There are great differences in performance characteristics. No one model is universally best. All reflect the designers' preferences and maximize certain features at the expense of others. The decision about what you want is yours alone, depending on your abilities and the way in which you plan to use the boat. This chapter is intended to lead you through the somewhat bewildering dimensions of sea kayak performance and design.

There are kayaks designed specifically for the ocean. Others are designed for more general use but are serviceable on salt water, such as the Folbots of

The three boats in the foreground are Eskimo and Aleut
skin kayak designs from Greenland and Alaska. Like the two
modern sea kayaks in the background, many contemporary models
are strongly influenced by these traditional craft.

The Nordkapp, a popular sea kayak in the narrow British tradition

South Carolina (their catalog depicts matronly Folboters cuddling miniature poodles among Cypress Garden lily pads as well as athletic paddlers on the ocean). Still other boats handle well in calm seas, but have serious drawbacks if the going gets rough.

The choice of boat is a matter of weighing performance against such other considerations as air transportability, comfort, speed, load-carrying capacity, and cost.

What constitutes seaworthiness is a controversy that polarizes sea kayakers into two schools of thought. The advocates of wider, but somewhat slower and less responsive craft base their preference on the stability that comes with higher hull volume and greater beam. Opposing them are the proponents of "high-performance" kayaks: narrow-beamed, faster boats that attain rough-water agility through the paddle strokes and balance of the kayaker.

Kayak Features

STABILITY

Kayaks differ greatly in the ease with which they capsize. Some will flip with only a slight shift of the paddler's weight; others allow you to stand up

The Orca's twenty-five-inch beam makes it one of the more
stable and highest volume sea kayaks.

without capsizing. Generally, the greater the stability, the slower the boat.

Low stability is a hazard unless you are skilled at Eskimo-rolling a boat fully loaded with gear and have watertight deck sealing. At sea, the ability to recover from a capsize is an absolute must, either by rolling upright or making a "wet exit," swimming out of an overturned boat. On a river or small lake, a kayaker usually can land and bail out the boat after a wet exit. But in the north Pacific, cold water, tidal currents, and distance to shore will probably force you to make an in-the-water recovery.

A more stable boat has a lot going for it. You need not devote as much atten- tion to keeping it upright and can get into the cockpit more easily. Further, you can rummage around down below with less concern for shifting your balance, rest if you are seasick or exhausted, or reach for things in the water. All these things can be done in boats not as stable, but with much greater reliance on your paddle.

Width of the hull is the most important factor in stability, though hull cross- sectional shape contributes in a minor way. Round hulls are quite unstable; hulls with a moderate V bottom and a hard chine (an angular ridge along each side below the waterline) tend to be more stable. A modified round hull with a somewhat flattened bottom also provides fair stability and is most typical in sea kayaks. Wider hulls (more than about twenty-three inches beam for a single- seat boat) provide a measure of large-angle stability: they can maintain equi- librium when tipped partway over and the paddler's weight is shifted. This built-in protection against going over the rest of the way provides a second to brace with the paddle or recover your balance. In narrow-beamed boats, there is no significant large-angle stability (regardless of hull shape) to compensate for the paddler's shifted weight as the boat tips. More than a few degrees of tipping mean you are going to go over unless you counter with a paddle brace.

Some sea kayaking experts argue that a narrower hull is more stable in steep seas, and that wider, flat-bottomed boats tend to be thrown over on their sides by steep, broadside waves, while a paddler in a narrow boat will be able to balance and brace himself upright in the same situation. Others claim that wider boats are at no disadvantage to such broaching waves.

Some kayaks feel extremely tippy with only the paddler aboard. They have low initial stability because the waterline is narrow when lightly loaded, but have good large-angle stability when heeled over ten degrees or so. Most of these boats feel much better when loaded with enough gear to bring their fuller beam down into the water.

TRACKING

Some kayaks travel as straight as an arrow and are very hard to turn. Others are always trying to turn (such as the average white-water boat that will turn sideways and stop within a few seconds after you cease paddling). On the ocean, the ability to hold a course is generally more important than maneuverability, as covering straight-line distances is the most usual situation, with few obstacles requiring tight turns. Sidewinds or waves often push the boat off course, but boats that track well are less susceptible to those influences. A kayak with good tracking is much more restful to paddle because it covers some distance in the appropriate direction between strokes and is less likely to need paddling on one side to compensate for wind or waves.

The underwater shape of the boat from end to end affects its tracking or turning. Boats which have a keel-line profile curving upward toward bow and stern (a "rockered" bottom) will turn more easily; a flat bottom profile will resist turning. However, a boat without a rockered bottom that is loaded a bit too heavily in the bow will tend to yaw from side to side, making slow turns that are very hard to correct or prevent.

Many sea kayaks have a moderately rockered bottom but gain tracking ability from a rudder or a skeg (a nonsteerable fin). When the skeg or rudder is cocked up above the water (using a line from the cockpit), the boat becomes considerably more maneuverable. These kayaks are good all-round craft for use on flat water and also on moderate white water where more agility is important (though they have much less maneuverability than a white-water boat).

Skegs can be a disadvantage in following waves or surf, as the skeg gives the boat a tendency to broach (turn sideways to the waves), which could be disastrous. When the waves are not directly from astern, more paddling on one side is required to stay on course.

A few sea kayak manufacturers claim their boats need no rudder for steering, maintaining that the hull form tracks well enough without it. The real test

*The Sea Otter is designed to need no rudder and is considered
to work quite well without one in most conditions.*

is a quartering wind, as most kayaks that track well will still tend to *weathercock*
(turn into the wind) and require far heavier paddling on the windward side to
hold a course. This occurs because the center of resistance to sliding sideways
in the water is forward of the center of resistance to the wind. Kayaks with
peaked bows and sterns usually are more inclined to weathercock than are
boats with low ends. (A few kayak makers claim to have balanced the wind and
water forces well enough to prevent weathercocking, and say that their boats
can be paddled easily on any course regardless of the wind direction.)

SPEED

Some kayaks simply move more easily than others. Actual speed differences among kayaks are not great, perhaps four knots rather than three.
That can mean covering twenty miles a day rather than fifteen. But more important is efficiency, the amount of energy needed to maintain cruising speed,
affecting how long you can keep it up, how often you have to rest, and how far
you can paddle to windward without approaching exhaustion. Some kayak brochures advertise that fifty-mile days are possible, but the endurance of the paddler's posterior seems more important than the kayak's attributes for that sort
of marathon. Ease of propulsion is, nonetheless, very important on any
extended trip.

A kayak's efficiency of movement and its speed are dependent on a variety
of technical factors, some of which have meaning only to naval architects. It is
not easy for the inexperienced eye to judge a boat's efficiency by looking at it;

trying it out is really the only effective test.

Speed and efficiency depend most heavily on waterline length. Wider, shorter boats usually are slower than long, narrow ones. The area of wetted surface on the submerged hull is also a factor, due to friction. Round hulls have the least wetted surface for a given volume of hull submerged in the water. Thus, hard-chined or flat-bottomed hulls tend to be less efficient than round hulls.

Turbulence and waves created by the boat's motion contribute drag. Having the widest portion of the hull aft of center (a "reverse fish-form" or "swede-form" hull) and a sharp stern area below the waterline seem to minimize this resistance in shallow-draft hulls like those of kayaks. However, "fish-form" hulls (widest portion ahead of center) can also be quite efficient, particularly at slower speeds.

Narrow Boats, Wide Boats, and Seaworthiness

The debate between the "fast-and-narrows" and the "wide-and-stables" continues. The narrow boats trace their roots to British designs like Derek Hutchinson's Anas Acuta. Its present-day North American descendants are models like the Nordkapp, the Umnak Icefloe, and the Mariner. All reflect the British approach to sea kayaking—a boat that will look after you if you look after yourself. Stability depends on the paddlework of the kayaker. Constant vigilance and a well-honed Eskimo roll are the first and last line of defense in these boats. Without these skills, in the opinion of some narrow kayak advocates, you do not belong out there on the water.

Many highly experienced ocean voyagers disagree. Finesse with the paddle is valuable, but a boat should be seaworthy in its own right, making capsizes less likely. Though wider boats are harder to Eskimo roll, the potential need for the maneuver is greatly reduced. Proponents of wider boats maintain that there is nothing inherently more seaworthy about the narrow boats, and that they are far less so in inexperienced hands or with an incapacitated paddler. In regard to lasting ability in stormy waters, John Dowd put it to me this way: "Your plump old Folbot is more seaworthy than any Nordkapp. You'll still be snoozing in the bottom of yours while the 'high performance' boy has just failed to complete his hundredth Eskimo roll."

My personal preference is for a wider and more forgiving boat, but I will not deny that many kayakers would be happier in a narrow boat. For stronger and more adventuresome people who may want to race or cruise a little faster and farther, a Nordkapp, Heron, or Mariner is fine. The important thing to recognize is that such boats place more responsibilities on you. You must have well-developed skills before heading for open water. This means practicing countless paddle-braces in order to have skills that will allow you to respond reflexively to any possible upsets, rather than to panic in the face of them.

These responses only work when the paddle is in hand, and there are times

The Mariner's narrow beam and long waterline length give it speed and paddling efficiency, at the expense of stability.

when it will not be. For instance, while he is bottom fishing, a kayaker's line hooks on the bottom, the kayaker pulls for all he is worth, the line frees, and he goes over backwards. Then, all the intricate self-rescue techniques are a poor substitute for a stable boat.

Wind Resistance Versus Dryness

The shape of a kayak above the waterline affects how much the wind pushes it around and how well it sheds waves. *Windage,* or the amount of surface area presented to the wind, significantly affects paddling to windward and the boat's tendency to veer off course in crosswinds. Boats with low profiles and less windage also tend to be wetter, since waves sweep over the hull much more easily. With a spray skirt, this presents no hazard, but it does cause discomfort (and may require wearing a wet suit).

Drier boats are definitely more comfortable. You can travel in calm weather with the spray cover unzipped or removed and have access to items kept below. In lower boats, you run the risk of being swamped in even slightly choppy conditions if the spray skirt is removed from the coaming (cockpit's rim).

The height of the cockpit above the water (referred to as freeboard) and the upper hull's shape affect the path of waves splashing aboard. Peaked decks shed water more readily before it has a chance to wash back to the cockpit. Rounded side decks allow waves to wash up to the cockpit more easily than a vertical hull side meeting a flatter deck in a sharp corner. But boats with more vertical sides and flatter decks are more difficult to paddle since the paddle blades have to clear the corners.

The shape of a kayak's bow can produce a drier ride to windward and also reduce resistance to pushing through waves. Many of the newer sea kayaks' distinctive peaked bows are designed with these considerations in mind, but again, there is little agreement about how well they work. A bow that flares above the waterline tends to deflect water sideways and downward. The peaked bow provides some reserve buoyancy (volume above the waterline), which is designed to help the boat rise over waves rather than knife through them. There is some debate about which way of taking the waves is best. The rising bow makes for a drier ride, as fewer waves sweep back along the deck. But the force of lifting over waves detracts from forward momentum and may increase pounding of the hull, which has the same detrimental effect. Knifing-bow advocates also argue that the reserve-buoyancy bows do not have enough backup volume to do much lifting. They also point out that the peaked reserve-buoyancy bows increase the windage.

Very low bows have one potential drawback—they could catch kelp. When you are paddling through a kelp bed in rough water, it is easy for a low bow to dip under the surface, so that you are suddenly wearing two or three heavy kelp hoses across your lap (with a good chance of being spilled, if you are struck side on by a wave). Since these kelp strands can be a hundred feet long, the only practical ways to get out are to cut them or back out.

The ability to handle surf or run downwind with large following seas requires characteristics that conflict with some of the attributes we have discussed. For surfing (going with the waves' direction of travel), a rockered bottom seems best to prevent the bow digging in and causing the boat to veer off and broach, but rockered boats do not track as well. A knifing bow is considered best for launching into surf, as a bow that rides over will slow the boat and make it more likely to surf backward.

*The peaked bow on this Umnak Icefloe helps to part waves
and aids Eskimo rolling by making the kayak less stable upside down.*

EASE OF ESKIMO ROLLING

The easier a kayak is to Eskimo roll, the easier it is to capsize. The wider, flat-bottomed hulls are very difficult to roll. As these hulls resist capsizing, they also resist being rolled back up. Many sea kayaks are designed to ease rolling upright. Peaked ends or a raised deck area forward of the cockpit make the boat unstable upside down and assist slightly in righting it.

Even more important than hull shape is bracing to keep the paddler in place in the seat. Without good knee and foot bracing, you simply fall out of the cockpit when the boat is upside down. Without good bracing on the side of the seat, you slide sideways when the boat is halfway up, which will prevent finishing the roll successfully.

HULL VOLUME AND CARGO CAPACITY

The volume inside the hull limits how much you carry with you. Internal space is limited and too much weight overloads the boat, with loss of seaworthiness and efficiency because the hull sits deeper in the water than it is designed to do. Low volume is the primary drawback of white-water boats for anything beyond a weekend trip.

The main difficulty in many kayaks is that storage space is broken up into long, thin, and hard-to-reach locations. For instance, there is a great deal of elongated volume in the ends of the longer touring fiberglass kayaks; things have to be pushed up there one at a time with a stick. Then, how do you get them out? This requires either tying retrieval lines to them before insertion or installing a round, screw-in Pyhi-type hatch (commonly available at marine supply stores) in the forward deck through which you can push things in and out.

Many sea kayaks have a bulkhead forward or aft of the cockpit (or both), creating watertight compartments that provide flotation and keep your gear dry if you should capsize and bail out. Some are reached through a fiberglass hatch; others have screw-in hatches that are watertight but will not accept large or long things, which means that tent poles must be stored on the deck or in the cockpit. All hatches leak to some extent when submerged, though the screw-in ones are the most watertight.

A bulkhead aft of the cockpit and a hatch on the rear deck of this Sandpiper provide a watertight compartment should the rest of the boat become flooded.

In the folding kayaks, storage spaces are broken up by the internal plywood frames. Access is via the holes through the frames. Inflatable boats have so little internal volume that storage is negligible.

Storage atop the deck in waterproof bags or boxes is an alternative, but a less-than-desirable one. It significantly raises the center of gravity of the boat, making it more vulnerable to the effects of wind. But on long trips or in less commodious boats, it may be the only choice.

Weight distribution fore and aft affects the boat's performance. Fortunately, most boats have equal storage space forward and aft of the cockpit. A little arrangement of what goes where can trim the boat as desired. The worst situation is a boat that tends to concentrate too much weight forward, with detrimental effects on steering and handling waves.

The Cockpit

How good you feel in your kayak is just as important as how well it performs in the water. Sea kayakers usually spend far longer stretches in their boats than do river runners. (River kayaks become uncomfortable fast.)

The most important consideration is the seat. There are many styles, and none is inherently better. Some kayakers feel a seat that raises you a few inches off the bottom of the boat is more comfortable, but others prefer to keep the center of gravity lower and sit on the bottom. Any seat should support you down to midthigh. Either a hard contoured or a padded seat will do, but you should be able to drain or wipe dry either one so you will not be sitting in a puddle or on a damp sponge. The seat needs a low back, probably no higher than a few inches above the belt. (Folbot seat backs are too high and sometimes give me back pains and stomach cramps.) A low seat-back also allows you to shift your weight more easily.

Your legs should be extended forward, slightly bent. There should be room to flex them occasionally. Many kayaks have a padded knee-brace area under the deck.

The only adequate way to test a kayak for comfort is to stay in it for more than an hour. Any kayak will feel good for the first few minutes.

Single- or Twin-Seater Kayaks

Single-seat kayaks are also called K-1s and twin-seaters, K-2s. The choice comes down to a matter of preference. Two singles have more cargo space than does one double-seater. Together they also weigh more than one double, which may be significant if you are looking at folding boats and thinking in terms of air transportation costs. I have heard couples say that they started with a double

The Beluga by Easy Rider

boat and then went on to two single ones, tired of being "Siamese twins." Single boats offer much more freedom to explore on your own and to get away from fellow travelers when you want to. After a week or so with a group, being able to go off for a short solitary paddle has some appeal. Double boats are cumbersome to paddle alone and harder to carry by yourself.

There are, however, advantages to doubling up in one boat. The per-person weight of the boat is less and paddling efficiency is increased, due in part to the longer waterline. If the two paddlers are unequal in strength and stamina, paddling a double boat makes it easier to travel together since their efforts are "averaged" and they stay together. In rough water, it is reassuring to have a larger boat—and company aboard.

Safety considerations cut both ways. In the case of a capsize, one single boat could rescue another more easily than could a capsized double effect a self-rescue. However, if one person were disabled, the other person could get him to civilization more easily in a double boat. But then, he could go for help more easily in a single.

Folding Kayaks

Folding kayaks are extremely strong, flexible, and seaworthy craft that have earned their reputation in ocean expeditions worldwide. They crossed the

The Klepper Aerius II

Atlantic on two occasions. John Dowd, author of *Sea Kayaking,* has made major ocean voyages well out of sight of land in his Klepper.

Of course, the primary reason for owning a folding boat is to gain air-travel mobility. (Sea kayak designer Werner Furrer maintains that is the only reason to have one.) But if you live in an apartment, a folding kayak is the one kind of boat that will not insist on being your major piece of furniture.

Four major companies manufacture folding kayaks suitable for ocean travel and available in North America.

Klepper of West Germany and Folbot of South Carolina both make single- and double-passenger models that pack down into two or three packages per boat. One bag contains the longer, narrower members (including paddles) and is about five feet long and a foot in diameter. Another holds the fabric skin and frames in a more rectangular package about two feet or more on a side and a foot or so thick.

The Klepper is the Mercedes Benz of folding boats. The Folbot is not as costly, about five hundred dollars less than the Klepper. The single and double Kleppers (the Aerius I and II, respectively) are considerably lighter than the Folbots, somewhat narrower, and less stable. Because the Kleppers rely on internal air bladders for skin tension and emergency flotation, they have less cargo capacity than the Folbots.

The Kleppers are better engineered and are built from superior materials. Folbots are more difficult to assemble (requiring some shoving and stressing of

Assembly of the Klepper Aerius II

the materials); each assembly of the boat wears it out more. Klepper parts go together cleanly with little forcing, and hull tension is added last by inflating the air bladders. The Folbots get their skin tension by tightening fasteners around the cockpit; these can be <u>extremely</u> difficult to engage in cold, rainy weather when the hull fabric is stiff. The newer Folbot fabric hulls are of a lighter and more perishable material and many have a wrinkly fit on the deck (mainly a cosmetic problem).

You pay your money and take your choice. Folbots are definitely seaworthy, but you will have to accept more wear and maintenance along with the boat's tubbiness and additional weight.

John Dowd operates Ecomarine Ocean Kayak Center in Vancouver, British Columbia, and is importing some interesting folding kayaks not available elsewhere in North America. He has a military version of the Klepper Aerius II.

The French Nautiraid is a double kayak which Ecomarine carries. Design and price are similar to the Klepper, but hull tension does not depend upon the lateral air bladders. Nautiraid also makes a sinister-looking, dark gray military version that self-heals bullet punctures.

East Germany makes the Pouch folding kayak, available in single or double models at Dowd's store. The design, quality of construction, and price are similar to the Folbots. Some of the structural members seem a bit undersized. Dowd suggests a number of relatively simple modifications the purchaser could make that would greatly improve the Pouch kayaks.

The Nautiraid

Fiberglass Kayaks

The greatest variety of sea kayaks is available in fiberglass. (More than thirty models were being manufactured in the Pacific Northwest in 1982.) A highly versatile material, fiberglass can be utilized in a combination of fabrics and resins with significant differences in strength, flexibility, weight, and cost. Since manufacturers base a good deal of their sales pitch on their boats' construction, you need some knowledge about fiberglass materials and kayak construction methods.

TYPES OF FIBERGLASS

Fiberglass is a generic term applied to a lamination of fabric and resin. Most sea kayaks are made of glass cloth, mat (a nonwoven sheet of fibers), or roving (a heavy, coarsely woven material). A sandwich construction, with a layer of foam material such as core-mat or Airex, may be incorporated in the bottom of the boat for rigidity. Layers of these various fabrics are saturated with resin and may be coated on the outside with gelcoat, a smooth pigmented resin.

The least expensive resin is polyester, which produces a strong lamination with moderate flexibility and is used on many of the sea kayaks. If the lay-up is made from a good combination of fabrics and a proper balance of resin, polyesters are more than adequate for the stresses and abuses to which most sea kayaks are subjected (generally not as great as those in white water).

Many sea kayaks now are made from vinylester resins, which are more flexible than polyesters. They also can be used with the new "miracle" fabrics, including Kevlar (used to make bulletproof vests) and graphite fibers. Those products are extraordinarily resistant to puncturing and are widely used in white-water craft. The cost of those fabrics also is extraordinary. Vinylester resins cost more than twice as much as polyesters; Kevlar and the like raise the cost even more. Vinylester resins in conjunction with conventional glass fabrics seem worthwhile in sea kayaks due to the added flexibility, but normal ocean kayaking conditions do not justify the cost of Kevlar or similar fabrics.

Epoxy resin is not necessarily stronger than vinylester, although it is more expensive. At present, few sea kayaks are made from epoxy, which is hazardous to work with. However, it is useful for repairs on polyester or vinylester hulls.

PROBLEMS IN FIBERGLASS KAYAK CONSTRUCTION

The proper balance of resin in the fabric lay-up is very important for strength. Too little resin results in dry spots in the lamination that reduce strength; too much resin produces brittleness and added weight. Most professionally built kayaks have properly controlled resin content, which can be further ensured by a process called vacuum-bagging. The lay-up is done normally, but then the inside of the hull is covered with plastic sheeting and a strong vacuum pump applied beneath it while the resin hardens. This spreads the resin more evenly and also reduces air pockets and bubbles within the lay-up. If you are purchasing a kayak that has been laid-up by an amateur without vacuum-bagging, look for uneven resin content from the inside of the hull. The light transmitted through the lamination will show light or dark patches if this prob-

Vacuum-bagging at Eddyline Kayak Works

lem exists.

Flat-bottomed kayaks may flex on the bottom, an effect called "oil-canning." Since fiberglass is flexible, oil-canning is not a serious defect, but it is disconcerting in rough water and certainly does not help the boat's performance. Round-bottomed hulls do not normally suffer from the problem.

As long as the hull can flex inward when it hits something (such as a submerged rock), it is unlikely to fracture. But an internal bulkhead or other stiffener can make the hull more vulnerable to cracking. If a boat runs aground, indenting the hull in the process, a fracture can occur just ahead of the bulkhead. Such "hard spots" can be corrected by stiffening and thickening the entire bottom, as with a core-mat sandwich. Some kayak builders put a very thin bulkhead in their boats on the premise that it is better for the bulkhead to break than the hull.

Inflatable Boats

Most inflatables belong in swimming pools. They are fine as shore tenders for sailboats, and some can handle moderate white water. But only a few are adequate for ocean travel. Most can be guaranteed to float. They are of rugged material that is not easily holed, and even if filled with water, they still will support passengers. But they will not carry much cargo, have little freeboard, will not track, and are abominations in wind.

However, Metzeler of Germany makes the Riverstar (double model) and Spezi L (single) which are very tough, decked boats capable of taking what the ocean dishes out. They are reasonably light and pack into a smaller package than the folding kayaks. They will not carry much inside the hull besides passengers, though, and do not track particularly well (though they are fitted for foot-steered rudders). Furthermore, they are almost as expensive as the Kleppers, and unless you want something equally well suited for white water, I do not think as good a buy.

Canoes

In 1976, three canoes paddled the entire Inside Passage from Vancouver, British Columbia, to Glacier Bay, Alaska. These open aluminum canoes, covered by homemade, fabric spray decks, survived the whirlpools of Dent Rapids and a rough crossing of Dixon Entrance. They were not the first nor will they be the last canoes to complete the twelve-hundred-mile journey.

The characteristics desired in an ocean-going canoe are the same as those of a kayak. Foremost, it must track well, which usually means the canoe has a keel strip. Most of the decked canoes (C-2s) currently available are designed for white water and track poorly.

Accessories

Spray Covers

Every ocean-going boat—canoe or kayak—must have a means of sealing the cockpit around the passenger to exclude breaking waves, spray, and rain. Both comfort and safety are involved. There will be situations in which you simply will be too busy paddling to bail. There will be other times when spray, wind, and rain will make the snug spray cover a comfort indeed.

Kayaks likely to be Eskimo rolled should be equipped with a spray skirt that fits tightly around both the wearer and the cockpit. The material usually is neoprene or a similar rubbery substance. Since the cockpits of these boats are small, the spray skirt is worn by the paddler (hence the term "skirt") and attached after entering the boat. It does not provide for ventilation and does not allow easy access below decks while in place. These skirts usually are bought

*Some people feel that decked canoes,
such as this one, are suitable for sea travel.*

to fit the boat. They can be altered by gluing new seams.

The more stable folding kayaks with more freeboard usually have a spray cover designed to shed water rather than to withstand immersion during rolls. Zippers generally are used to close the opening around the paddler, allowing easy access below. (Waterproof zippers designed for divers' "dry suits" work well.) The covers made for the military Klepper and Nautiraid boats are excellent, combining a fixed spray cover and a spray skirt worn by the paddler. The standard spray skirt for the Kleppers and those available for Folbots are not very good, as they leak badly.

Since the folding boats lack a flange around the cockpit, spray covers usu-

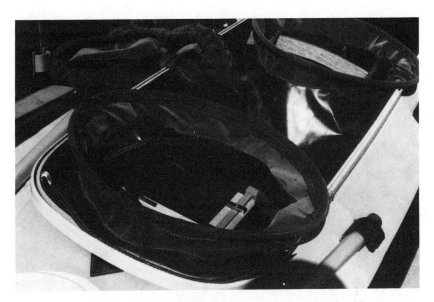

The Nautiraid's two-piece spray cover has a removable skirt.

ally are secured with snaps, and waves taken over the side can squeeze under and into the boat. The big, open cockpits also require reinforcement of the spray skirt against large waves taken over the deck. These can be in the form of removable plywood deck pieces that support the cover above the paddler's lap.

Shoulder straps are nice to have on any spray cover that separates readily from a capsized boat. They keep it high on you without the need for an uncomfortably tight waistband (which can be made adjustable to close up tight when you need it). Keeping the spray cover up just below the armpits does a lot to protect you from spray.

Paddles

The length of paddles depends on the boat, but they should be much longer than those used in white water. Most sea kayakers prefer a length between seven and nine feet; longer paddles are better for wider boats to give clearance over the decks, and also seem to add speed.

Such paddles may be jointed in the middle for ease of transportation and storage, though many people do not like them because the joint tends to loosen with usage. The joint allows the two shafts to be twisted and may be set so that the blades are parallel or at right angles to each other (feathered). Some paddles have a locking device to keep the blades at the degree of twist you want; these are much better than those without the lock, which tend to twist gradually.

The blades are the most delicate part, and those of wood are susceptible to

Touring paddles usually range from six to eight feet
long. This model breaks apart in the middle and can be set with
the blades feathered or unfeathered.

splitting. Paddles with laminated blades (some even with a layer of aluminum between wood) are difficult to obtain, but much more durable. There are a number of excellent fiberglass paddles (such as those made by Eddyline or by Werner Furrer in Seattle) which may cost more than one hundred dollars.

Drip-rings—rubber sleeves that slide onto the shafts of jointed paddles—are very worthwhile. They intercept water that runs down the shaft from the blade as each one is raised, making the water drip over the side of the boat rather than run down to your hands and lap.

A spare paddle, secured to the deck, should be carried in every boat. If a paddle is dropped, the spare can make the critical difference between retrieving the lost paddle or being carried away from it helplessly. A small, single-bladed paddle is sufficient in most cases.

With the advent of the new fiberglass paddles, the likelihood of breaking a paddle at sea is less than with wooden ones. But to be on the safe side, you might want to carry a spare two-bladed paddle instead of just a single-bladed one.

RUDDERS

A rudder is worthwhile on any boat on which it will fit and in which feet can be used to steer. A steerable rudder allows all paddling energy to go into propulsion rather than steering, which can be significant in side winds or when weaving through obstructions. Rudders add little drag and give little interference in landings if they can be raised (cocked).

Some kayakers detest rudders, maintaining that properly designed kayaks do not need them. *Seal launches* —a means of entry from rocks by which a kayaker in his boat is dropped bow-first by someone else—cannot be done with a rudder. Rudders are one more thing to break. One paddler told me of hopelessly entangling his rudder in a kelp bed, saying he would have had to leave his boat to disengage it if someone else had not been present to cut him free.

I have never had problems with entanglement. My rudder has always ridden up and over kelp or other debris. It is possible to back up through kelp if the rudder can be cocked high enough above the water.

Both rudders and foot-control kits are available from a number of kayak makers for boats that do not come equipped with them.

SAILS

Full sailing rigs, including leeboards and enough sail area to tack to windward, do not seem appropriate for long coastal trips. Conditions are rarely favorable for windward sailing on the North Coast, where "feast-or-famine"

Rudder in cocked position, clear of water, kelp, or rocks

A "pusher" sail for downwind sailing

winds generally seem the rule. In even moderate winds, sailing a kayak or canoe to windward is just too risky. A spill could be fatal. Too often the cumbersome rig is carried along unused.

But a small "pusher" sail for downwind sailing is very worthwhile. It can be small, needs no elaborate rigging or leeboards, and is much safer to use. The spars can be made from materials found along the way and are easily stowed on deck when not sailing.

I use a small, square sail that can be fitted either to a mast or the end of a paddle. I prefer to use a separate mast in order to keep the paddle handy (to prevent broaching in following waves, for example) and often paddle while sailing in light wind. The bottom of the boat must be fitted with a mast socket (a one-inch hole in the keel of a Folbot, or a drilled block glued into other boats). The mast can rest against the forward edge of the cockpit coaming, tied in place if necessary. The sail and lines should be located so that they do not interfere with paddling and can be released quickly. The cross-spar at the top of the sail fits into a sleeve. The sail can be stowed by rolling it around the cross-spar and the mast carried on deck, secured through loops attached to the cockpit coaming or under shock cords elsewhere on the deck.

*This sail rig allows paddling under sail. The bow at center
provides quick release of the sail in an emergency.*

KITE-SAILING

Using kites as a means of going downwind recently has become popular for both canoes and kayaks (Eddyline of Everett, Washington, sells two sizes). Aside from just being fun to fly, kites have some advantages over sails. It is easier to fly a big kite than to rig a big sail. Since a kite flies higher than a sail, it catches the steadier and stronger winds aloft. Kites do not block your view or impede paddling the way sails can. Because a kite is attached to the kayak through the paddler's hand or a deck cleat, heeling force is less than for a sail on a mast and spills therefore less likely. Depending on your boat's tracking ability, you probably can sail up to thirty degrees off to either side of the wind direction.

But after using both sails and kites, I still like my sail better. Launching a kite is an operation that takes at least two hands (while you also hang onto the paddle and watch your direction). If the wind is fluky, the kite may drop to the water during lulls, and you have to pull it all in and start over. The bigger kites will fly only in more than ten knots of wind (and need more once you get going downwind, reducing the apparent wind), whereas sails work to some extent as long as there is any wind. Retrieving a kite and its line from the water can be messy, especially in a kelp bed.

Equipment
Afloat and Ashore

In this chapter you will find a long list of items you may wish to take. Sea kayaking, particularly on the remote, damp North Coast, calls for quite an array of equipment. Some of it is essential; most is simply nice to have. Though many kayaks are cavernous, it is easy to overload yourself, usually causing discomfort in the boat before loss of seaworthiness. You will regret lugging too much stuff in repeated and sometimes distant hauls between low tideline and camp. Few kayakers, myself included, carry all of the items listed here, but I have met people who consider one or more of them to be essential. In the Appendix is a checklist that notes what I consider optional. Decide for yourself, considering both safety and comfort.

Clothing

Kayaking on the North Coast demands more specialized clothing than do recreational activities in other settings. Though summer temperatures are pleasantly warm, dampness is a fact of life. Take lightweight pants of a polyester-cotton blend. They dry quickly, whereas denim jeans will stay wet indefinitely in damp weather. I have some old Forest Service pants that can go from completely soaked to totally dry in little more than an hour! Also, avoid pants with a flat-felled seam at the back, as these can become very uncomfortable while you sit in the kayak. Shirts that are a blend of wool and synthetic are a good compromise between fast drying and warmth. A light, "breathable" but water-repellent jacket is comfortable to wear on fair but windy days when you may get spattered with spray and paddle drips. Also bring a wool hat.

For additional warmth, a sweater and vest prove more than adequate for summer trips along the coast. The vest should have a synthetic insulating layer rather than down, which loses its insulative properties when wet and is very difficult to dry.

FOOTWEAR

You will need two sorts of footwear, one in which you can wade and another for hiking around ashore. For the latter, standard hiking boots are not much good because the woods are often wet. Once leather boots get wet, they are very difficult to dry.

There are almost as many points of view on footwear for wading as there are ocean kayakers. Most everyone who paddles on the North Coast agrees that you need something to keep your feet either dry or warm while wet. Very few wade barefoot or use the sandals or sneakers used by river runners because the water is too cold for comfort. Having cold, wet feet for a long period of time in damp and stormy weather is unpleasant.

Many ocean kayakers wear wet suit bootees and carry some standard footwear for use ashore. The bootees keep your feet warm (though not dry) and provide some protection while wading. I tried them, but concluded that they cannot stand up to much walking on rough and barnacle-covered rocks, and I dislike the clammy feeling of tightly covered wet feet (though they do stay warm enough).

I am an advocate of dry feet while wading. Some "dry-foot" proponents like three-quarter-length (thigh-high) waders that can be rolled down for walking, though these can be dangerous in a spill from a kayak because they fill with water. Rubber knee boots (the ubiquitous "gumboots" worn by everyone on the North Coast) do a fine job and allow you to wade plenty deep enough for kayak launching. Ashore they're a bit clumsy and uncomfortable for walking very far.

Two approaches to sea kayaking footwear: rubber knee
boots (left) *or wet suit bootees* (right)

(Felt innersoles make them much more comfortable.) Boots with smooth soles designed for wearing aboard sailboats are not the best choice because the soles do not stand up well to wear and pick up pebbles. Boots with a heavy welt and lugged soles last longer and make for easier walking on beaches or steep terrain.

Another alternative is a boot with a molded-rubber shoe (to ankle height) and leather upper, of the type introduced by L. L. Bean as the "Maine hunting shoe." Liberally waterproofed with SnoSeal, these withstand immersion above the ankles with only slight leakage. Since they lace up tightly, water does not flood in if you do go in over the top. By changing socks and felt innersoles in the boots, I find my feet stay comfortably dry. These boots are far better than gumboots for hiking ashore. Bring along a high quality bicycle tube repair kit for patching rubber boots. (Duct tape works temporarily.) I prefer canvas (not leather-trimmed) sneakers to wear in camp. Others swear by the moccasin or oxford-style version of the Maine hunting shoe.

RAIN GEAR

Both a raincoat and rain pants are vital equipment. Genuine foulweather gear for marine use is the most watertight and durable. Foul-weather gear is also useful for pushing through brush (especially salal) in damp weather, so it should be tough enough to resist tearing. Bib overalls are more comfortable than waist-high rain pants. The overalls, worn over a shirt but without a coat, will keep you quite dry ashore, and will protect your lap from drips while paddling. A sou'wester rain hat is more comfortable to wear than a hood and, worn backward, doubles as a sun hat.

GoreTex rain garments do not seem to work on the North Coast. Whether the fabric is affected by salt or simply overwhelmed by the seriousness of its

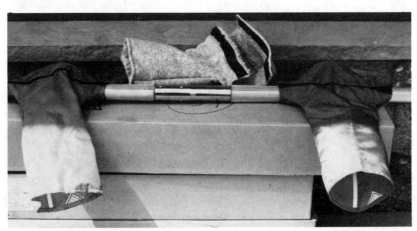

Pogies and optional liner

task is unknown; it just leaks. No one I have met who brought GoreTex to this rainy country has been happy with its performance here.

You may want some protection for your hands against the cold, wet weather and against paddling blisters. To keep hands warm and dry, "Pogies" (mittens that fit over the paddle, available from most kayaker suppliers), latex household gloves, or rubber fisherman's gloves all work well. Sailing gloves may serve you for blister protection, though I prefer to put adhesive tape on particular spots before they get sore. One of my paddling companions swears by fast-drying spandex driving gloves.

Camping Gear

I am assuming that readers of this guide are experienced campers, so any comments here refer only to the special demands of North Coast camping. Both a tarp and tent are highly desirable; the uses of a tarp are detailed in the chapter entitled "Making Yourself At Home." The tent rainfly should provide good protection against driven rain all the way around, and should have well water-sealed seams.

Since summer temperatures rarely drop below the midforties (below five degrees Celsius), a medium-weight sleeping bag is sufficient in the summer. Synthetics like PolarGuard are better than real down, since the former dry better and are warmer when damp. Once damp, a down bag is likely to stay that way unless you have the luxury of a day of sun in which to spread it out.

Cooking gear is standard. A good Teflon frying pan is very nice for frying fish. A stove is an asset for getting quick starts in the morning or for brewing tea or soup during a lunch stop and is essential in the treeless upper reaches of Glacier Bay. White gas is available at most towns along the coast.

For food, you can choose any combinations of freeze-dried meals, dry and canned goods from the grocery store, or your own concoctions of bulk items. Take food out of its packaging and put it into one-quart Ziploc bags, where it will stay drier and take up far less room. I have had little trouble with food spoiling on the humid North Coast. On a long trip, package each of the items susceptible to moisture in several small bags and work from one at a time.

Camera Protection

For years I have carried an old Pentax Spotmatic camera with me on coastal kayak trips, with no significant damage to it. When I recently had it

Box found on the beach becomes kitchen counter.

cleaned, the repairman said he could see no major evidence of saltwater corrosion. Surely it is a risk to carry a camera in an ocean kayak, but with some precautions it can survive indefinitely.

Saltwater immersion ruins a camera unless it can be taken to a repairman in less than forty-eight hours. (Immersing it in fresh water will not help.) Short of dropping it overboard, the main hazard is a capsize or flooding the boat. You will need to have a durable, waterproof container in which to keep the camera. A rigid, watertight box, such as a military-surplus ammunition can or one of the specially designed waterproof plastic boxes available at kayaking or river-running suppliers, will provide excellent protection. I have used the SportsPouch, an inflatable pouch designed for cameras, which has a sealable opening and takes less room in the cockpit than a box. However, it did not prove to be as durable as a box; the seams eventually ripped.

The camera also must be protected against salt spray or drips from your paddle. I never use my camera on the water in windy weather and always put it back in its container after I take a picture. While wearing the camera with a neck strap, you can slit an inverted plastic bag and slide it down the straps to cover the camera until you want to snap a shot.

Compass

Many kayakers mount a marine compass on the deck just forward of the cockpit. This has the advantage of always being available when you need it. Also, the compass is aligned with the boat's fore-and-aft axis so that you merely need to read your course under the pointer or *lubber line*. But as the compass is used only occasionally, I feel that a small hand-held compass designed for hikers or orienteers is sufficient. It should have a mirror and sighting device for taking bearings on distant points. Since marine charts use magnetic directions, there is no need for an adjustment in the compass to set declinations to true north as with topographic maps. The compass can be slipped into the chart case where you can see it as you paddle along.

Nautical Charts

Charts of the North Coast are usually available at marine suppliers in the Puget Sound area (such as Captain's Nautical Supplies in Seattle, which carries a good stock of the entire coast), and in most coastal communities in northern British Columbia and Southeast Alaska. General stores in the smaller North Coast towns and even larger fish-buying scows usually carry charts for their local areas. But since charts are useful for trip planning, you will probably want to get them before you leave home. If they are not available in your area, they can be ordered.

United States charts may be obtained from the National Oceanic and Atmospheric Administration (NOAA) and Canadian charts from the Canadian

A hand compass secured in the map case is adequate for most kayak navigation situations.

Hydrographic Service at the addresses listed in the Appendix. Ask for NOAA Nautical Chart Catalog 3 (Alaska) or Canadian Catalog 2 (Pacific Coast), either of which also includes instructions for ordering. The Tidal Current Tables for the Pacific coast (which covers both Alaska and British Columbia) also can be obtained from NOAA.

Kayak Flotation and Dry Storage

In case of a spill a kayak requires air bags, which are placed in its hull, or bulkheads to keep it afloat. When packing goods and equipment for a long trip, there is, of course, no room for air bags. However, the waterproof bags in which you pack your gear will trap enough air to provide flotation for the kayak. Most bagged gear will be less than half as dense as the same volume of water and will provide plenty of extra buoyancy so long as water is kept out of the bags. Special dry-storage bags (made by Voyageur, Phoenix, and other manufacturers) inflate to fit tightly in the boat's storage space, or you can use heavy garbage bags or trash compactor bags (the latter work very well). Two bags, one inside the other, should cover critical items, with each bag tied off separately. The bag should be twisted shut, doubled over, and then tied up tightly with cord or sturdy twist-ties. To protect the plastic bags from pinholes and rips, slip them inside duffel bags. As further insurance of both flotation and dryness, individual items or small groupings of clothing and foods should be bagged separately in half-gallon or quart-size Ziploc bags.

In the case of a spill, things will slosh about inside the boat and may wash out the cockpit. To make sure you do not lose your flotation/gear, wedge in or

A Type III life jacket

otherwise secure the bags. (The internal frames in folding boats will help to keep things in place.)

Safety Equipment

First-Aid Kit

The first-aid kit should include items necessary in any wilderness setting. A strong painkiller (preferably the kind prescribed by a physician and with a long shelf life), butterfly closures (in place of stitches), seasickness pills (Bonine is said to produce less drowsiness than others), and a general-purpose antibiotic pill (probably also prescription) are worthwhile additions.

Life Jackets

A life jacket must be comfortable for paddling and sitting in the kayak, and must not be so long as to interfere with the boat's spray cover. Not all jackets are suitable. The best is the Type III PFD (Personal Flotation Device), one of five categories approved by the U.S. Coast Guard. The Type III is like a vest, with a zipper in front, and foam flotation sewn into narrow vertical pockets or large flat panels in front and rear. Most kayakers like the narrow-strip version, as it is more flexible. Type III life jackets are made by a number of manufacturers. Some have pockets in which flares and survival items can be carried; if not, these can be sewed on.

The Type II PFD, worn by the paddler on the cover of this book, is horse-shoe-shaped, fits around the neck, and ties in front and under the arms. Though the Type II provides adequate flotation and does not interfere with paddling, it can chafe the neck. Most sea paddlers prefer the Type III.

Wet Suits

Wet suits provide good insurance. They greatly reduce the risk of hypothermia and help to keep a spilled kayaker afloat. However, they are uncomfortable to wear and cannot readily be put on in a kayak or in the water. If you carry one, wear it in such hazardous situations as long crossings or rough weather. The sleeveless, "Farmer John" type is not sufficient for cold northern waters; get one with long sleeves and legs, and made of material a quarter-inch thick.

Exposure Suits

The bulky exposure suits, also called *walrus suits,* give very good long-term protection in cold water. Most commercial fishermen carry them, and the

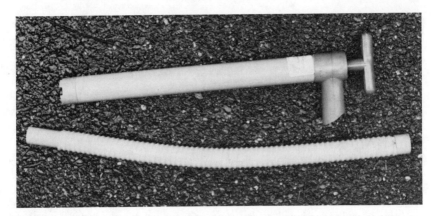

Bilge pump and extension to help eject water over the side
rather than back into your lap

suits have been credited with saving many lives when boats went down. A crab-boat crewman wearing one is reported to have survived twelve days in winter waters of the Gulf of Alaska. Unfortunately, you cannot paddle while wearing a walrus suit. But it can be rolled up small enough to stow alongside the paddler in the cockpit of a wider boat and easily can be donned (even in the water). You can swim (after a fashion) in it. Good exposure suits are made by Imperial of Bremerton, Washington, or Bayley of Fortuna, California. Many marine suppliers carry them. The cost is about three hundred dollars.

Bilge Pump

Though hand bailers are very effective in removing large quantities of water from a boat, bilge pumps are more effective for bailing in rough water, as you can pump out the boat with the spray cover closed up, which can make a critical difference in rough water. The Umnak Icefloe and the Nordkap kayaks have built-in pumps mounted on the deck. For other boats, there should be a hand-held pump with the capacity to move at least eight gallons per minute. The plastic Thirsty-Mate pumps work well. Secure the pump with duct tape or Velcro inside the cockpit so it will not be lost in case of an upset. A short hose extension is handy for getting the discharge over the side of the boat.

Emergency Signaling

Because of the long daylight during summer months, orange smoke devices are a more appropriate choice than flares. Be sure you have the type that can be hand held; some must be set on a fireproof surface. Aerial flares, such as Skyblazers, shoot up a hundred feet or more and burn for up to ten seconds. I usually carry both smoke and aerial flares, taping a flare to my life

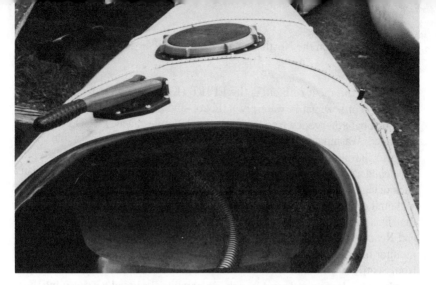

Deck-mounted bilge pump located behind the cockpit

jacket and another one plus a smoke device inside the boat's cockpit.

Smoke or flares should be used only when there is a boat or airplane in sight less than a mile or two away. In most areas, you're likely to see a fishing boat or low-flying floatplane at least once a day, and the Canadian and U.S. Coast Guards fly the outer coast at least once a week. But when an area is closed to commercial fishing or when you are in a remote area, you may not see potential help that often. For that reason, radio signaling devices are worth considering.

Signaling devices (left to right): *two small aerial flares,
a hand-held flare, and an orange smoke device*

One of the most reliable is the EPIRB (Emergency Position Indicating Radio Beacon), which is waterproof, floats, and emits a continuous signal on international emergency frequencies up to 250 miles away. EBCO Products of Redmond, Washington, makes an EPIRB designed for small boats (but a little large for kayaks) that sells for about two hundred ninety dollars. EBCO has developed a personal model with less power and duration, slightly larger than a pack of cigarettes and retailing for about one hundred fifty dollars. It floats and will emit a signal for up to forty-eight hours. When the transmitter is activated, the signal may be received by U.S. or Canadian military or Coast Guard Search and Rescue aircraft in the area, or more likely by commercial aircraft which monitor the emergency frequencies whenever flying over water (such as flights from Seattle to points in Alaska).

In 1982, the Soviet Union launched a satellite designed for receiving these signals and relaying them to the nearest search-and-rescue station. It successfully located a downed aircraft in British Columbia, pinpointing it within twenty meters! A similar satellite was launched jointly by the U.S., Canada, and France in 1983. These alternative sources provide very good insurance that your signal will be picked up anywhere on the North Coast (or elsewhere).

Small two-way VHF or Citizens' Band radios are available, but expensive. Fishermen often use CBs for informal communication, but a VHF is more reliable for emergency communication and even can be used to place telephone calls anywhere in the world via the marine operator, if you are so inclined. ICOM of Bellevue, Washington, makes a twenty-five-watt, twelve-channel set which is only seven inches long, weighs about a pound, and costs about five hundred dollars. A set of that kind has a range of about ten miles at sea level.

SURVIVAL KITS

What happens if you have to abandon your boat and swim to shore in remote country? You will be a prime candidate for hypothermia and may then have to survive for weeks before rescue. As remote as the possibility may be, it is worthwhile to ensure that you have some vital items stowed on your person to enhance your chances of survival once you get ashore. John Ince and Hedi Kottner, authors of *Sea Kayaking Canada's West Coast*, report that such a kit saved the lives of two kayakers marooned on the west coast of the Queen Charlottes.

Warmth and fuel for your body will be the immediate problems, making waterproof matches and fire starter the fundamentals of your kit. Since combating hypothermia also requires a food energy source, include a good supply of dextrose tablets or some similar source of easily metabolized carbohydrates. You probably will be able to find a can of some sort on the beach, so it would be possible to boil water, and some tea or bouillon cubes would be a nice asset. Plastic bags large enough for you to crawl inside will help to prevent heat loss. Be sure to include at least one flare or smoke emitter and a multipurpose knife.

The kit can be worn in a modified nylon money belt, surplus Air Force survival kit vest, or in pockets sewn onto a life jacket.

Folding and Fiberglass Boat Repair

BOAT REPAIR

Duct tape is the standby for quick but amazingly durable repairs to all kinds of kayaks. I have patched small holes in my Folbot with duct tape that lasted for the duration of the trip without further attention. It sticks well underwater (but the surface must be dry when you apply it) and is very strong. I usually put a strip around the outer edges of my Folbot at the beginning of each trip to prevent abrasion and to stop the small leaks that otherwise occur there.

FOLDING KAYAKS

Though these boats are complex, a small kit can repair almost any problem with the hull skin or internal structural members. Be sure that you have the proper patching material and glue for your hull (for example, the Hypalon hulls on Kleppers). Pliobond works quite well on vinyl Folbot hulls, though it produces unsightly discoloration. For small holes caused by barnacle abrasion or pebbles trapped inside the hull under the keel, an application of Pliobond is usually enough. Almost any broken structural member can be repaired with a splint reinforced with epoxy cement and a few wraps of duct tape. Breaks in the aluminum tubing longitudinals can be fixed with a short dowel carved from a cedar branch and inserted into either end of the break. Broken fittings are a more difficult problem. Carry a few items of hardware (nuts and bolts and a small turnbuckle) and a small roll of annealed (soft) wire to deal with these as best you can.

A small pair of vise-grip pliers with wire cutters will be a great asset in repairing a folding boat. They can be used to hold a drill bit, a hot nail for burning holes in wood, a sail needle for heavy-duty sewing on the boat's skin, or a piece of hacksaw blade while cutting metal.

With all folding boats, watch out for gravel or pebbles that get under the keel pieces. When the boat is dragged over anything, these protrude and easily can wear a hole through the hull. Check for them periodically, and disassemble the boat to remove them as needed.

FIBERGLASS KAYAKS

Fiberglass boats are the least likely to need repair. But, as with folding boats, duct tape is a first line of defense for most small punctures. For more durable repairs, a small epoxy kit is good insurance. Epoxy will adhere to both polyester and vinylester resins. Avoid the hardware store's multipurpose kits, which include more chemical properties devoted to shelf life than to adhesion. Cold-Cure epoxy or a similar product is better. In addition to the two-part epoxy resin, carry a piece of standard fiberglass cloth and a piece of mat (unwoven fiber sheet), a piece of coarse-grit sandpaper, and a small brush. For a punctured hull, sand both the inside and the outside thoroughly (especially the outside, sanding through the gelcoat, if any), brush on resin, then mat (pushing it down well with the brush), followed by cloth well saturated with resin. Do this both inside and outside and allow the resin to harden fully, at least overnight.

Planning a Trip
to the North Coast

Pretrip planning is a real source of enjoyment and discovery as you gather information and form impressions of your destination. Such an exercise is both useful and satisfying as you hone your ability to imagine faraway places with some accuracy. That skill can serve as a kind of divining rod, leading you to routes and places that suit you and helping you to avoid disappointments.

If you wish to follow the routes suggested in the second part of this book, the information in this chapter will be useful in deciding which trips to take and how much time to allow for them. Contrary to what many first-time visitors believe, the North Coast is a tremendously varied place, with diverse climates, landforms, vegetation, and patterns of human settlement.

Sea Otter Sound, Alaska

*South Prince of Wales Island, Alaska, looking
west toward Dall Island*

Pick Your Setting

THE OUTER COAST

On the Pacific fringe are the wildest, most varied, and dramatic elements of the North Coast. Marine life is richer there than on the inland waterways, beaches are longer and beachcombing at its best. The pinto abalone is found only in this zone, on rocks and reefs washed by ocean swells. Islands are more rugged, with sea caves, arches, and extensive reefs hiding tiny coves with miniature and rarely visited beaches. Though settlements are fewer on the outer coast, fishing boats (especially trollers) are common offshore or at anchor in quiet bays. Fish-buying scows occupy the better anchorages near popular fishing grounds from midsummer to early fall.

The outer coast offers the most challenging and diverse paddling conditions. Pacific swells always are present, and even light winds kick up enough chop to slow a kayak's progress. The rounding of capes or points can demand hard paddling to fight strong winds and confused seas. But I also have spent entire windless days lazily paddling miles offshore, rising and falling on swells resembling glassy, gentle hills.

Rocky, broken coastline permits you to slip through the protective cover of offshore rocks, kelp beds, and small islands, paddling in reasonably serene waters only yards from the ocean's tumult. Tidal currents rarely attain enough velocity to be an important consideration on the outer coast.

Smooth and unbroken coastline means hard going for kayaks, with difficult paddling and few opportunities for shelter. For instance, I would not want to travel the coast between Lituya Bay and Yakutat in Alaska—about fifty miles of uninterrupted beach, with the only exit from the water through heavy surf. I also avoid coastline composed of series of headlands and deep bays, as the former are obstacles that get tiresome and can upset a traveling timetable with unpredictable waits for reasonable weather. Fortunately, broken coastline is common in both British Columbia and Southeastern Alaska.

Most of the North Coast's outer fringes (including the west coast of Vancouver Island) is a mix of large and small islands which offer alternative routes—protected channels winding among the islands or open-ocean travel outside when the weather permits. Thus, you usually get a nice mix of ocean and flat-water experience. There are other areas where frequent open-ocean exposure is unavoidable—the west coasts of Dall Island and Baranof Island to name two. Because of their exposure and vulnerability to bad weather, sea kayakers are rare on those coastlines.

INTRAISLAND WATERWAYS

The Inside Passage stretches from behind Vancouver Island to Skagway, Alaska, with only two stretches exposed to the Pacific. It is a progression of narrow channels, wider straits, and occasional sounds into which ocean swells penetrate. These waterways may be as flat as a millpond (and hardly as wide from shore to shore) or have rushing tidal currents (some with powerful rips, overfalls, whirlpools, and even riverlike white water). Crossing the larger of these bodies of water can be as challenging as the open ocean. But the true Inside Passage—the north-south route followed by the Alaska and British Columbia ferries—is a very small portion of an extensive network of protected waterways. To both the east and west of the main corridor are many more which are far less frequently used. The east side of the Queen Charlotte Islands offers a similar setting. Though facing on huge Hecate Strait (with the mainland well out of sight on the other side), the eastern side of the Charlottes is largely protected from ocean swells.

Progressions from narrow waterways to large inland bodies of water and back again provide a diverse and interesting paddling environment. Though paddling generally is easier than on the outer coast, heavy seas may be encountered on the larger sounds and straits. Pleasant beaches abound on the wider waterways, with plentiful campsites (though driftwood for fuel is less plentiful than on the outer coast). Since the inland waterways are the primary routes for maritime traffic, settlements and industry are more common there than on the outside. Shacks, cabins, and floating dwellings (not all inhabited) are likely to be found wherever the shoreline affords protection for small boats. The remains of canneries and salteries (most of which were burned after abandonment) are scattered along the waterways. Active logging is extensive along parts of the

Float-house in Tenakee Inlet, Alaska

Inside Passage (especially in Southeast Alaska) and on northern Moresby Island in the Queen Charlottes.

Because marine traffic and settlements are concentrated on the inland waterways, arrangements for travel are easy to make. There are countless options for paddling between communities with surface or air travel connections. A kayak trip can be started and ended at the same community, making a loop so that you will not paddle the same waters twice. A variety of routes permits some paddling on the outside coast as well as on the inland waterways.

INLAND FJORDS

Most of the North Coast is fringed with inlets running deeply into the coastal mountain range. Most of the inlets are no more than a mile wide, but run up to hundreds of miles inland from the Inside Passage. The country is spectacular, with steep mountainsides plunging thousands of feet to sea level. Gigantic rock walls and cascading waterfalls abound. In places, whole mountainsides have slid into the fjord, trees and all.

Since most of these fjords dead-end deep in the mountains, where road access is impossible, the deeper you penetrate, the wilder they get. Many of the mountainsides are too steep to be logged. Some inlets have small Indian communities at their upper ends. For an intimate impression of the fjord country and its people, read Margaret Craven's *I Heard the Owl Call My Name.*

Though these fjords are more like freshwater lakes than the sea (and some really are predominantly freshwater due to river influx or glacial melt), they still can present rough paddling. Air drainages run up or down them (usually from seaward in the summer), meaning you may encounter stiff headwinds or tailwinds. Occasionally, large air masses in the mountains will spill into a fjord, creating very strong winds called *williwaws.*

Campsites in fjord country may be scarce because of the rugged terrain, with the only flat spots at side drainages. Driftwood is very hard to find in this fjord country, but alder thickets provide plenty of fuel near the shoreline.

Southeast Alaska or B.C.?

There are some interesting physical and cultural differences between the Southeast Alaska and B.C. coasts. Climate varies greatly within each region.

Vegetation changes as you travel northward. Sitka spruce, western hemlock, and cedars dominate the forests of the coast in both B.C. and "Southeast," as most Alaskans call this state's lower panhandle. The nature of the underbrush is important to those who seek access to the shore. On the outer coast of B.C. and the southernmost part of Alaska, salal can present an almost impenetrable barrier, as much as six feet high. Sometimes the only way through it is on hands and knees or over fallen logs. Salal can eliminate camping at what would otherwise be ideal spots. On B.C.'s inland waterways and in the eastern Queen Charlottes, salal is less of a problem. In most of Southeast, the salal is far less common, giving way to more unobstructed forest floors, open muskeg, and meadows of grass and heather (although on Southern Prince of Wales Island, salal, huckleberry, devil's club, alder, and fallen trees can produce a jungle in which it is impossible to camp).

Both Southeast and B.C. have a history of development and commerce much more active than that of the present day. In the early part of the century, canneries and mining flourished. Most of those commercial sites have been abandoned, but in many coves, you will find traces of those activities if you look carefully. Southern Prince of Wales Island and Moresby Island are especially rich in such history.

Many defunct communities still are shown on B.C. maps (especially on road maps that no one has bothered to update for the roadless coast). For instance, Wadhams, once a cannery town, now is inhabited only by two caretakers. Jedway was an open-pit mining community. Now everything is gone but the scars. Searching about in the salal for Allison Harbour, I was unable to find any trace of settlement.

Southeast has many small settlements, some of which have withered to

*A whaling station in the Queen Charlotte Islands, which
operated until World War II*

single-digit populations, and some of which recently have revived. There still
are a few ghost towns, including a mining community that once boasted two
hundred residents.

Climate

In general, the North Coast is a very rainy place. Annual precipitation on
the westernmost edge averages about 100 inches. But climatic conditions vary
tremendously within the region. Skagway, for instance, gets only 26 inches of
precipitation a year. By contrast, Vancouver Island's Barkley Sound is the wet-
test place on the north Pacific coast, with 262 inches a year. Little Port Walter,
on the southern end of Baranof Island in Alaska, is not far behind with 221. But
just thirty miles south of Little Port Walter, Cape Decision gets only 76 inches,
and fifty miles northeast, Kake gets a mere 57. These differences are important
to note in planning a trip if you wish to avoid rain. Tables 5-1 and 5-2 summarize
weather conditions for selected places during the summer.

Moisture-laden storms approach the North Coast from the west, coming
out of the Gulf of Alaska and dropping rain as they pass the outer coast. A great
deal more is released as clouds rise over higher land masses. The mountains of
southern Baranof Island are a prime example. It is estimated that more than

TABLE 5-1
SELECTED CLIMATIC CONDITIONS IN
SOUTHEASTERN ALASKA DURING SUMMER MONTHS

Place	Month	Average Temperature (Fahrenheit)		Average Rainfall
		Maximum	Minimum	(Inches)
Yakutat	June	56	42	6
	July	59	48	8
	August	60	46	11
Skagway	June	65	45	2
	July	68	49	3
	August	65	48	3
Gustavus	June	61	44	3
	July	62	48	5
	August	62	47	5
Juneau	June	62	44	5
	July	64	48	7
	August	62	46	7
Cape Spencer	June	54	46	6
(Cross Sound)	July	58	48	7
	August	57	48	9
Five Finger Lighthouse	June	58	47	3
(Frederick Sound)	July	59	50	5
	August	59	49	6
Sitka	June	59	44	4
	July	62	48	5
	August	62	49	7
Wrangell	June	62	47	5
	July	65	50	5
	August	63	49	6
Davis River	June	61	44	4
(Portland Canal)	July	63	47	5
	August	62	47	5
Ketchikan	June	62	48	7
	July	65	51	9
	August	66	52	12
Hydaburg	June	65	46	5
(Southern Prince of	July	68	51	4
Wales Island)	August	70	51	7

Note: Data on number of days with rain or fog and predominant wind direction were not available from the *United States Coast Pilot.*

TABLE 5-2
SELECTED CLIMATIC CONDITIONS IN
BRITISH COLUMBIA DURING SUMMER MONTHS

Place	Month	Average Temperature (Fahrenheit)		Average Rainfall (Inches)	Days with Rain	Predominant Wind Direction	Days with Fog
		Maximum	Minimum				
Ivory Island (Milbanke Sound, Central B.C. Coast)	June	58.2	48.6	3.26	13	W	3
	July	61.3	51.2	3.65	12	W	7
	August	62.5	51.3	5.59	13	SE	6
McInnes Island (Laredo Sound, Central B.C. Coast)	June	58.8	49.2	5.30	15	S-NW	2
	July	62.0	52.2	2.86	13	NW	6
	August	62.9	53.7	5.82	16	NW	7
Cape St. James (South Queen Charlotte Islands)	June	55.6	47.3	2.91	15	NW	8
	July	58.4	50.2	2.74	14	NW	12
	August	60.5	52.6	2.68	14	NW	11
Sandspit (East Central Queen Charlotte Islands)	June	58.4	48.8	1.88	13	SE	1
	July	62.2	52.6	1.85	12	SE-W	3
	August	63.5	53.6	2.05	12	SE	2
Masset (Northeast Queen Charlotte Islands)	June	60.7	46.1	2.70	14	—	—
	July	63.6	49.9	2.69	13	—	—
	August	65.2	51.2	2.89	14	—	—
Langara Island (Northwest Queen Charlotte Islands)	June	55.1	46.4	3.24	18	—	6
	July	58.5	50.3	3.41	18	—	9
	August	60.0	51.9	4.30	18	—	8
Prince Rupert (North B.C. Coast)	June	59.6	46.6	4.27	16	SE	2
	July	62.5	49.9	4.62	17	SE	6
	August	63.4	50.7	5.87	16	SE	6

three hundred inches of annual precipitation falls in the peaks just west of Little Port Walter! Lower land and water on the lee side of the mountain range enjoy the rain-shadow effect, with much less precipitation. Kake is an example of that. The sequence can be repeated (with less dramatic extremes and gradually decreasing precipitation) as the storms move inland. This pattern—moderate precipitation on the outer coast, highest rainfall around and just beyond mountainous country, and reduced precipitation for a distance to the east—occurs all along the North Coast.

The steep topography and major waterways divert weather flow, greatly affecting local conditions. Wind directions generally conform to topography. (Note the B.C. differences in predominant wind directions in the table.)

Fair weather usually brings west or northwesterly winds, especially on the outer coast. Stormy or rainy weather usually is accompanied by southeasterly winds which switch to southwesterly as the disturbance moves past. But on the inland waterways, winds can come at you from any direction.

Temperatures vary slightly along the coast during the summer; parts of Southeast are warmer than the more southerly B.C. coast. The areas with less precipitation usually are also the warmer ones. Night temperatures during the summer rarely drop below forty-five degrees Fahrenheit, so a fairly light sleeping bag should suffice. Sea temperatures average about fifty degrees in early June, rising to about fifty-eight in August.

All things considered, June and July are preferable to August, since there is less rain and more daylight earlier in the summer. Note the monthly patterns in the tables for the areas that interest you, as they do vary. Gales and rainy weather increase toward the end of August, so September is a much less desirable time to be on the North Coast. Vancouver Island, however, usually enjoys mild weather through that month.

Planning with the Tides

Tides and their accompanying currents affect a trip as much as does the weather. In areas where currents are strong, travel must occur when favorable ones are going your way. Though tides are generally greater to the north, the narrow channels of inland waterways squeeze the volume of water to produce greater effects. For example, Sitka, on the outer coast, has a maximum range of about fifteen feet. Inland to the east, Juneau has a twenty-five-foot range! A greater tide range means carrying your boat and gear longer distances at low tide. I have sometimes had to go a quarter-mile to get to the water at low tide from a campsite only a few feet above the high-water line.

Current strength is not necessarily related to tide range. The strength is most dependent on the degree of constriction imposed by the waterway and how much water is backed up behind. National Oceanic and Atmospheric Administration (NOAA) current tables cover the entire Pacific coast, giving the times of change and speeds. Since currents may run as much as hours behind changes in the tide, a current table is far more useful than a tide table, although both are worth having.

There is merit in trying to plan around the monthly tide cycle, which corresponds to the phases of the moon. The highest tides, called *spring tides,* give the best access to intertidal marine life on the corresponding minus tides. Spring tides also mean the fewest campsites on or near the beach. Once, during such a tide, we camped in a grassy meadow in Lisianski Strait south of Glacier Bay, only to discover that night that the meadow had flooded with several inches of seawater.

Picking Your Route

Having decided on a general area to visit, you will want to work out the specifics of where to go. Picking starting and destination points will narrow the options, but there still are likely to be a variety of channels or island complexes from which to pick. You will want to study the route for potential campsites, open-water crossings, and characteristics that will affect the amount of time you will want to allow to cover it.

At this point, I usually purchase the most detailed charts available. If you are going a long way or if the charts do not happen to coincide with your route, this can get expensive, and you may opt for small-scale and less detailed charts. The large-scale charts (scales of about 1:20,000 to 1:40,000) are well worth the expense, as they show the details so important to the coast-hugging kayak: tiny coves and passages, rocks, beaches, kelp, and the like. In areas of complex islands and offshore rocks, smaller-scale charts generalize features to the point of uselessness. You actually can get lost in such areas without a good chart to keep track of exactly where you are. And the ability to spot a tiny high-tide passage from the chart may save miles of paddling.

How Far to Go in the Time You Have

How far you will be able to travel in the amount of time you have depends on your endurance, your boat, and how you want to divide your days between paddling and staying ashore.

Weather will be an important factor. I have found about one day a week unsuitable for traveling due to stormy weather. During that same week, you can expect one day of on-and-off rain, one day of overcast (perhaps with rain for a short while), and a day of at least some sun with no rain. I generally travel farthest on partially rainy overcast days, which are not too uncomfortable and do not make exploring ashore as tempting. Really rainy and blustery days tend to be short-distance days, if I travel at all. Sunny days do not see me covering much distance as a rule, since the sun makes beaches and islands all the more appealing. On such days, I often make camp early in a particularly attractive place and either do things ashore or take day-trips in the kayak, returning to camp in the evening.

I have found that I like one layover day in each four or five, depending on the weather. These layovers help break the routine, allowing time for doing laundry, cooking big breakfasts, hiking, taking day-trips in the boat, and simply resting from the nightly ritual of setting up camp.

Daily distances depend on your endurance—primarily that of your posterior. Some kayakers boast of fifty-mile days, but the most I ever have done was thirty. Even twenty miles is a long day, since that means spending at least five hours in the seat. In looking over my past trips, I usually have averaged about ten nautical miles a day (including rest days). Anything above that starts to take on the character of a marathon.

The nature of a route also affects how far you will be able to go in a given amount of time. Weather will hold you back more often on the outer coast than on the inland waterways. You will be able to travel farther in areas of broken shoreline with many sheltering islands than on more open coastline or channels. Crossings of more than a mile or two can significantly affect your schedule, as you may have to wait a day or more for suitable weather.

Getting to the North Coast by Land, Sea, and Air

Climbing ladder after ladder, we arrive at a glass-covered deck high atop the Alaska State ferry Columbia. *Open to the weather astern and carpeted with artificial grass, this is the solarium. Lair of the foot passenger, it resembles a Baghdad bazaar and a national gathering of the Rainbow Tribe, with all manner of Alaska-bound humanity settling in happy communion.*

Camping here are fishing crews heading north to meet their boats, New Jersey college students fresh off the Greyhound and hopeful of landing cannery jobs, adventuresome and outdoorsy grandparents, blasé Alaska residents, and clumps of federal employees. In the merry cacophony of boarding in Seattle, they scramble to stake out territories with sleeping bags and gear. The early birds pitch tents as private staterooms, securely anchoring them with equipment.

Later, as the scenic Inside Passage rolls by, kites fly, guitars

Kayak and Alaska ferry Columbia *at Wrangell*

plunk, pull-tabs pop, cameras snap. An impromptu group of musicians gathers, and twenty people dance a lurching Virginia Reel across the swells of Queen Charlotte Sound—a lively contrast to the more sedate territory of the stateroom passengers.

By Ketchikan, cards shuffle between diverse bands of passengers. Complete strangers have formed summer-long traveling pacts. The solarium is a celebration—an instant neighborhood.

Figuring out how to get there is part of the challenge of an ocean kayaking trip to the North Coast. There are many choices. This chapter describes the major transportation networks and compares the merits of different means of getting there with a kayak. Fares and tariffs are those current in 1982 and are reported in the currency of the respective country. Fares always are changing (especially air fares), but are given here to provide ball-park figures for estimating the cost of a trip and for comparing the respective costs of alternative plans.

As with most things in life, the cheapest way to the North Coast, by water, is also the slowest, and the fastest way, by air, is the most expensive. Ferry systems in both Alaska and British Columbia are well developed, and are an inexpensive means of transporting either rigid or folding boats.

Driving Your Car

Mountains and islands make the North Coast a region hard to penetrate by road. Because auto access to the coast north of Queen Charlotte Strait is so limited, it is an option I usually eliminate. The routes are roundabout and the roads sinuous, costly in both gas and time, making sea or air transportation much more attractive.

Not so on Vancouver Island. Good paved highways now provide access to both the southwestern coast and the northeastern area bordering on Queen Charlotte Strait and the many islands and fjords south of it. Route 19 from Kelsey Bay to Port Hardy was completed in 1979, cutting the better part of a day's journey by gravel logging road to only a few hours by smooth highway.

Primary access points for the outer coast of Vancouver Island are Ucluelet, Tofino, and six hamlets north of there which require lengthy approaches on gravel roads. The extensive gravel road system on Vancouver Island crosses heavily logged lands which are either owned by timber companies under a Crown grant or leased to them for forest management. Most of the roads were built by those companies and public use is by their permission. Roads are classified (and designated by signs) as either green, yellow, or red. The public can use green roads freely at any time. Using yellow roads means yielding the right-of-way to logging traffic. Red roads may be used after 5:00 P.M. weekdays and at any time on weekends. Many of the roads are very narrow, with room to pass logging trucks only at turnouts. Be careful.

North of Vancouver Island lies a hundred-mile stretch of coast where roads cannot penetrate the rugged Coast Range. Bella Coola is the first port beyond that to which you can drive. The approach is via one hundred miles of winding gravel road (with some spectacular scenery in Tweedsmuir Provincial Park). Bella Coola itself is about eighty miles from the open ocean. Narrow, steep-sided channels link town and sea. These offer fine scenery, but less of the diversity found on the outer coast.

Prince Rupert is the primary road-access point for the northernmost part of the British Columbia coast. Only forty miles south of the Alaska border, Prince Rupert is served by a fine highway, Yellowhead Highway 16. But the circuitous route into the interior makes it a thousand-mile drive from Puget Sound.

On opposite sides of the border are Stewart, B.C., and Hyder, Alaska. The towns are only about two miles apart. Stewart is at the head of the Portland Canal, a narrow waterway that runs one hundred miles southwest to the coast. Both towns can be reached by way of a thirty-eight-mile paved road, a turnoff from the Cassiar Highway. There is little reason for kayakers to head that way; there is too much narrow canal to paddle before reaching a change of scene.

Only two other communities in Southeast Alaska, Haines and Skagway, can be reached by road. The Haines Highway, paved only through the Alaskan portion, is well traveled year-round. Klondike Highway 2 to Skagway, partly paved and partly gravel, is steep and winding. These roads connect the Alaska Highway with the Alaska ferry system and provide good access to the Southeast panhandle—if you are coming from south central Alaska or driving the Alaska Highway. For those coming from the lower forty-eight states or from southern Canada, an eighteen-hundred-mile drive to Haines or Skagway is the hard way to reach the coast.

Ferries and Freighters

The least expensive way to get a kayak to northern salt water is by boat, primarily because there is no charge for excess weight (which quickly runs up the air fare). On the other hand, you pay the cost in time spent, a factor if your vacation is limited. You have to eat en route and ferry food is not the cheapest. But the ride provides a relaxing transition to and from your destination, and you will get a good feel for the coastal country. If you have a rigid kayak, the only practical way of getting it to areas not served by roads is by watercraft. In most cases (if you are traveling on a vessel), the kayak gets a free ride.

Baggage is not a problem on ferries that travel long distances and that cater to heavily laden foot passengers. If the load of gear is going to fit in your kayak, it should not pose a problem when you board the ship. But be reasonable; luggage is supposed to be what you can carry on, not a mountain of freight. On shorter ferry runs, used primarily by foot passengers who carry little with them, you are wise to get to the terminal early and consult the purser or deckhands about loading your kayak and gear with as little disruption as possible.

There have been major changes in marine transportation along the B.C. coast in the past few years. Because of the new highway to northern Vancouver Island, ferries that served the Johnstone Strait—Queen Charlotte Strait area no longer run. Gone, too, are fleets of little passenger-carrying freighters that plied the North Coast. These were expensive (passengers had to purchase a stateroom), slow (due to long stops for off-loading cargo), and often lagged far behind schedule. But the demise of those leisurely cruises, during which the outnumbered passengers mingled and dined with the crew, marks the passage of an era.

A much expanded B.C. ferry system now serves the larger coastal communities. Departing from Port Hardy, the ferry stops at Bella Bella, Ocean Falls, Prince Rupert, and Skidegate in the Queen Charlottes. Leaving Port Hardy at noon twice a week, the ferry reaches Prince Rupert early the next morning, and the far end of the ferry line that night. From Port Hardy, foot passengers pay $20 to Bella Bella, $30 to Prince Rupert, and $46 to Skidegate. Kayaks can be carried at no charge. You can purchase a berth or roll out your sleeping bag on a reclining deck chair. Bookings are made through B.C. Steamships in Vancouver (which also has a Seattle office).

There are a few short-distance water carriers serving the western coast of Vancouver Island. The *Lady Rose,* an eighty-foot excursion boat, stops in the

B.C. ferry Queen of Prince Rupert

Broken Group Islands in Barkley Sound, a popular place for kayaking. Operated by Alberni Marine Transportation, Ltd. out of Port Alberni, this venerable ship will carry passengers and kayaks to the islands for $12 and $10, respectively.

In Nootka Sound, there is the *Uchuck III,* a smaller ship that makes twice-weekly trips west and north out of Gold River (accessible by paved highway from Campbell River). Passenger rates top out at $16, varying with the destination. The fee for kayaks is $8, and kayakers can be dropped off almost anywhere along the route. (See Nootka Sound Service, Ltd. in Appendix.)

The Alaska Marine Highway, one of the most famous ferry systems in the world, is the prime carrier to and within Southeast Alaska. Owners of rigid kayaks rely on the Alaska ferry; those with folding boats enjoy it if they have the time. It serves twelve communities in Southeast, connecting with Seattle and Prince Rupert.

At present, rigid kayaks can be carried on the Alaska ferries at no charge, though on a space-available basis. They are stored on the car deck, under freight vans or wherever they will fit. If sea kayaking continues to grow in popularity, the ferry system may resort to a fee and reservation system for rigid kayaks. (Folding boats simply are stowed in the baggage carts.)

From Seattle, a deck passenger pays $105 to Ketchikan and $134 to either Juneau or Sitka. Staterooms and dormitory rooms also are available. They are more costly and require reservations months in advance. Leaving Seattle on Friday nights, the *Columbia* (flagship of the fleet) docks at Ketchikan early Sunday morning and continues on to other communities during the next forty-eight

Kayaks travel on the car deck on Alaska ferries (here beneath a trailer of frozen food).

The solarium aboard Alaska ferry Columbia

hours. There is a snack bar and also a restaurant on the *Columbia,* but meals are somewhat expensive (though a bargain by Alaska standards). Passengers may bring along their own provisions. It should be food that does not need cooking, as camp stoves cannot be used aboard. Deck passengers can sleep in the lounges, on the stern decks, or in the solarium.

Marine Highway ferries that make the local runs between Southeast Alaska communities are smaller but less crowded than the *Columbia.* Passengers are predominantly local residents. Some of those vessels have staterooms and dormitories; some do not. All have chairs and deck space on which to sleep. Showers are available on all ferries except the *Le Conte, Aurora,* and *Chilkat.*

Bumming a Boat Ride

There is always a chance of hitching a ride on a fishing boat, tug, or pleasure craft heading for the North Coast or operating there. I have begged rides on a number of occasions. At other times, rides were offered. Once, the skipper of a self-propelled fish-buying scow decided that it was too rough for my companions and me to paddle to our next destination. Since business was slow, he insisted that we load our boats aboard, then up-anchored and took us the whole ten miles, plying us with coffee and sweet rolls along the way and giving us a whole roast beef to take along for dinner. In Namu, B.C., the owner of a salmon troller decided to take another kayaker and me one hundred miles to Port Hardy. There he left his boat and took the jet with us to Vancouver, where he spent the weekend at his home. Such acts of generosity and hospitality help to make the North Coast a very special place.

You may be able to arrange a ride north from Seattle or Vancouver as a paying passenger or in exchange for cooking or other work on a fishing boat en route. Many boats head north with a full crew; they probably cannot accommodate you. Others go up short-handed, picking up their crews where they will be fishing. Those are the boats for which to look.

The fishing fleets usually leave Puget Sound between mid-May and late June. Generally, the gill-netters leave first, followed by the trollers and halibut boats. Seiners may not leave until the last week in June. This varies greatly from year to year, depending on the fishing seasons posted by the B.C. and Alaska regulatory agencies. Some boats headed for Alaska will make the journey nonstop, arriving in three or four days. Others take it at a more leisurely pace, stopping at favorite spots like Pruth Bay on Calvert Island. Many congregate in the shelter of "God's Pocket" in Queen Charlotte Strait, awaiting favorable weather to cross the Sound. Most boats stop at Ketchikan before proceeding to their Alaskan fishing grounds.

If you are carrying a folding kayak, it is best to keep it broken down. That minimizes the chance of its being damaged or getting underfoot. Rigid boats usually are stowed on the deckhouse or stern. Be sure they are securely lashed down, since in notoriously rough passages like Johnstone Strait, head seas may break clear over the deckhouse.

Do not accept tows for your kayak. Fishermen are used to towing skiffs, but kayaks do not tow well. They yaw from side to side, dart forward and ram the transom in following seas, and may even flip over. Your kayak may be gone or damaged by the time you discover that there is a problem and the towing boat slows down.

Air Travel

Scheduled airline and chartered floatplanes can get folding-kayak owners to their destination in the shortest time and with the fewest transfers. If time is your major limiting factor, air travel will be worth the extra expense (and you will not have to spend money on food or other sundries as you would if traveling by other, slower modes).

The speed at which aircraft can get you from city to wilderness can induce culture shock. For example, on a trip to the Queen Charlotte Islands, we left Seattle by airliner in the morning, connected with a chartered floatplane in the afternoon, and were standing alone on a remote beach by early evening.

Scheduled airline trips are easy to research and arrange. Travel agents have a book, the Official Airline Guide ("OAG" in the travel trade), that shows air service to just about any hamlet on the continent, revealing what outfit goes there, when they go, how much it costs, and what aircraft is used. This is a fascinating book to have. Since it is published twice monthly, it is easy to arrange for a travel agent to save an outdated one for you rather than tossing it. Though the information will not be up-to-the-minute, you can learn a great deal about who flies where and whether there is scheduled air service to particular villages. It also has some useful information on the characteristics of the assorted airplanes used for scheduled flights. The book does not include baggage allowances or charges, but a call to the airline can tell you that.

Most of the larger towns in B.C. and Alaska have daily jet service. Most smaller coastal communities are without runways and are served by semi-scheduled, amphibious airplanes that carry about a dozen passengers. Somewhat more expensive, they charge very high rates for excess baggage.

Alaska Airlines is the main carrier to and within Southeast Alaska. Excursion round-trip fares (requiring that you book a week in advance and stay at least through a weekend) are considerably cheaper than one-way fares. Excursion fares from Seattle to Ketchikan, Gustavus (Glacier Bay), and Cordova (Prince William Sound) are $225, $352, and $367, respectively.

In B.C., Pacific Western flies from Vancouver to Sandspit (in the Queen Charlottes) and to Prince Rupert. A round-trip fare to Sandspit from Vancouver costs $153. Air B.C. flies amphibians on scheduled flights to some, but not all, of the small communities on the North Coast. Those are more expensive than the jet flights. For example, a round trip to Bella Bella from Vancouver costs $264. Since the planes, Grumman Mallards, take only thirteen passengers, reservations made well in advance are a must. The luggage limit is forty pounds. Air B.C. will not guarantee that there will be room for excess baggage (at fifty cents a pound), and report that they often have to ship it on a later flight. They suggest you book an extra seat for your folding kayak to guarantee it space. Expensive indeed.

If you have a folding kayak with you on jet flights, chances are you will have to check some of your gear as excess baggage or air freight. Both Alaska and Pacific Western airlines allow two pieces to be checked. Alaska limits each piece to seventy pounds, with combined dimensions not exceeding sixty-two inches; Pacific Western's rules are tighter.

Carry-on pieces must fit under the seat (that means they must be less than nine inches thick). Think twice about what you put in your carry-on luggage. I once caused a commotion at the airport security check-in because I had thoughtlessly packed a short machete in my carry-on bag. After they decided I was not a hijacker, they checked it through specially for me.

Excess baggage charges usually are cheaper than air freight. Alaska Airlines will check up to four excess pieces at the following rates per piece: combined dimensions up to sixty-two inches and weight to seventy pounds, $8; combined dimensions up to one hundred inches and weight to seventy pounds, $12; and combined dimensions up to one hundred inches and weight to one hundred pounds, $35. Pacific Western charges $13 each for up to three excess pieces. For air freight, Alaska charges fifty-five cents a pound for up to seventy pounds, and then $39 per hundredweight. You must deliver it to a separate place with plenty of lead time, and understand that there is little likelihood that it will go on the flight with you. Pacific Western, by contrast, charges thirty-six cents a pound for air cargo and will try to put it on your flight.

There are things you can do to reduce baggage charges. Consolidate as much as you can to make up the fewest pieces (up to the maximum dimensions allowed), stowing sleeping bags and ground pads together in large duffels or in your boat bags (where they will act as padding for the folding-kayak parts). Perhaps you can talk a fellow passenger who is traveling light into checking one of your bags. This is not easy to arrange in the crush of big-city airports, but often I have done it on return trips.

Carrying firearms on airlines requires special arrangements. Pistols cannot be transported into Canada at all. Pistols and other firearms going to Alaska must be unloaded, broken down (if possible), and have the action locked open. They may be packed in your baggage or checked separately; ammunition must be packed separately from the firearm and carried in its original box. Flares may not be transported on airlines in either the U.S. or Canada. Buy them after you get there.

Packing Folding Boats for Air Shipment

There are two situations that present the greatest danger of breaking your boat. The first is dropping it while carrying it over slippery rocks or rain-soaked logs. All you can do there is be careful. The second is during air shipment on major airlines as baggage or air freight.

How you pack your boat can make a difference. After more than twenty flights, my single and double kayaks have yet to suffer any breakage. An adequate repair kit is the best insurance against a trip stymied by damage, but prevention is the place to start.

Tough bags are the first line of defense. Nylon pack cloth is preferable to cotton cloth because it will not mildew or rot while the bags are stowed away in the hull during the trip. A long zipper, preferably nylon, serves as the bag's closure, but the bags should also be well bound with rope or webbing.

You must pack the boat's pieces in the bags carefully. The paddle blades and plywood frames need special protection; pack things so that weight on the bag will not concentrate pressure on them. Include some padding: sleeping pads, seat cushions, life jackets, wet suits, wool jackets, and the like. Be especially careful to pad the corners and ends of frames and other parts that may be struck during handling. The fabric hull should be protected against

The De Havilland Beaver—the most suitable aircraft for two or three kayakers with folding boats. The bag on the forklift is a Folbot.

punctures. A sleeping pad spread over it in the bag plus a few articles of clothing should do the job.

Finally, pack the boat in two or three bags if possible. Keeping down the weight of each package is the best protection against breakage. This will also minimize loading problems in small aircraft.

AIR CHARTERS

Hiring a floatplane may be the only practical way to get yourself to certain remote spots. It is not cheap, but the convenience of being delivered to the point where you want to start paddling and the consequent time savings may offset the expense. Rates for air charters and how they are charged vary greatly, as do the loads that different air services will carry in the same type of aircraft. So, what is reported here should be taken as a general guide to what you should expect to pay. The key factor in determining cost is the type of aircraft.

Charter services usually operate any of four types of airplane: the Cessna (180 or 185), the De Havilland Beaver, the De Havilland single-engine Otter, or the twin-engine Grumman Goose. Payloads and operating costs of those aircraft vary significantly. These and other characteristics for each type of plane are summarized in Table 6-1, together with cost per mile (as of 1982) for chartering each type at four representative air services in different locations in

Washington State, B.C., and Alaska.

Note that I have included a range for the maximum number of passengers and payload of each aircraft. That reflects modifications to the airplanes and each company's load preferences. For example, some air services have wheels on the twin pontoons so that the floatplanes can use standard runways; these may subtract up to three hundred pounds from the payload of the bigger planes. On shorter trips, cutting the fuel load can substantially increase the payload.

Cessnas are only marginally adequate for two people with a double folding kayak and camping gear. Space is more of a limiting factor than weight; the tiny cabin fills up very quickly. Most air services maintain that two people and a kayak just will not fit in a Cessna 180, but two friends of mine were shoehorned in for a sixty-mile charter in Alaska. So it may depend on the service's willingness to load the plane to the gills (called *Alaska loads* in the trade).

The Beaver is the workhorse of almost every charter service, and the most likely candidate for most kayaking trips. Two passengers with a double folding kayak or even two single boats will fit in easily with plenty of camping gear. Three kayakers with single boats or a double and a single should make it, but four passengers with two double boats probably will constitute an overload.

For bigger groups, the single-engine Otter (there also is a twin-engine model) or the Grumman Goose would be more economical than two Beavers. Both usually can handle six passengers, their boats, and camping gear. The Otter is big enough to carry rigid kayaks in the cabin, though the lost passenger

Table 6-1
Aircraft Characteristics and Cost per Mile Reported at Four Locations

	Cessna	Beaver	Single Otter	Goose
Passengers (minimal luggage)	2-3	4-6	9	9
Payload (passengers and/or luggage)	500-600	800-1,100	1,600-1,800	1,800
Airspeed (miles per hour)	130	130	130	168
Cost per Mile (in US dollars) at:				
Seattle[1]	1.85	2.70	--	--
Port Hardy[1]	3.40	4.16	5.33	--
Sandspit[2]	--	3.79	5.01	4.96
Juneau[3]	3.16	4.76	--	--

[1]Reported in cost per mile.

[2]Reported in a combination of cost per mile plus cost per hour (converted by airspeed).

[3]Reported in cost per hour (converted by airspeed).

*The Cessna 180—only marginally adequate for two kayakers
and a double folding boat*

space would make that expensive indeed. The Goose is significantly faster than the other airplanes, due to its twin engines and boat-shaped fuselage (substituting for pontoons).

The only reliable way to find out exactly how much a trip will cost you is to ask a particular air service for a quote from point A to point B in a particular aircraft. Some services charge by the mile, including the mileage for the return trip of the empty plane (the *deadhead* trip). Thus, a rate based on one hundred miles means that you will be carried fifty miles for the price. In Alaska and B.C., hourly charges are the norm, although one air service in the Queen Charlotte Islands charges by the mile with an additional hourly charge to cover fuel (which fluctuates with current gasoline cost). In Alaska, typical hourly rates include the fuel cost.

Generally, the larger the party, the cheaper the cost per person of a charter. Based on an average of the charges reported in Table 6-1, the cost per passenger mile in a Beaver ranges from about $2 for two people to about $1.50 for three. Since a group of four may have to charter two aircraft (a Cessna and a Beaver), the cost per person rises to about $1.90 per passenger mile, so chartering an Otter (if available) would be more cost effective at about $1.30 per passenger mile. Costs for six passengers (the approximate load limit in the Otter for people, boats, and gear) decrease still further to less than $1 per passenger mile.

Some firms will give you a discounted rate (perhaps 25 percent off) if they can use the plane on the return flight. That is most likely to work if you are flying into a community or to a popular spot, such as a fishing resort, where

Interior of the Beaver, looking aft from the pilot's seat,
with both rear seats collapsed forward

returning parties are likely.

Most air services are extremely busy during the summer, and reservations should be made well in advance. A deposit of as much as 50 percent may be required. One firm in Juneau will refund your deposit if you cancel more than ten days prior to departure time.

Some air services in Canada will carry kayaks or canoes on the floatplane pontoons. Those in the United States now are prohibited from doing so. In B.C., one air service will carry pontoon loads only on their Otter; another will do it in the Beaver, but with only one passenger aboard. The reluctance results from disturbed aerodynamics, which make the aircraft hard to fly, the pilots nervous, and the insurance rates high.

Since you will most likely be flying to salt water, finding a big enough landing place should be no problem. It must be smooth water (the open Pacific is not suitable) and free from heavy chop. A lake may be used if the coast does not provide protected waters; takeoffs can get very interesting on these. At one popular hot spring in Southeast Alaska, a very small lake is used. Often passengers flying out are ferried, one by one, a few miles to a protected bay where there is room for the plane to take off with all aboard. At this pond, I watched a Beaver loading a few items for a Forest Service crew working in the area. The pilot was offered a small sack of garbage to add to the load. He refused the twenty-pound sack; the payload tolerance to make it off the lake was that close. The Beaver taxied to the middle of the lake and roared off toward the shore.

Then it spun in a 180-degree circle, spray flying, and completed its takeoff toward the other end of the lake.

Do not be surprised to have your flight delayed by weather, especially morning fog. Likewise, if you have arranged for a pick-up and the airplane does not arrive on time, chances are that weather has delayed it elsewhere. Stay there and wait.

You will not know how much you will be able to pack into a plane until you arrive at the air service office. That makes your charter costs uncertain if your load is borderline. Try to describe in advance what you will be carrying, but there is really no way for you to communicate the volume of it accurately. Most outfits often fly kayaks (especially in Alaska) and base their estimates on past experiences. Much also depends on the amount they are willing to jam into the airplane. If they say it will require a Beaver, you will just have to take their word for it.

Once all your transportation arrangements are made and paid for, you may look into your ravaged wallet and gasp. But if you take most of your food with you and can resist buying trinkets along the way, your expenses are taken care of. You may end up not spending much more than if you had stayed at home.

On the Water

My experience with North Coast paddling began with a long trip into some of its most remote country. Four of us in two folding kayaks paddled out of Sitka for thirty days' paddling along a hundred miles of outer coastline with nary a town. Our launching was inauspicious, a perfect showcase for a beginner's folly.

We chose an abandoned seaplane ramp from which to launch. The tide was out as we lugged load after load three hundred yards down the nearly level, eroded cement at the water's edge. We piled our gear like mountains next to the boats and began stuffing it in (a task we had never tried before), optimistically hoping we would find a spot for everything. For a long time, we stuffed and arranged, the piles of gear shrinking slowly, the boats' internal spaces filling quickly. Then we noticed that the incoming tide had nearly sur-

Kayaks off Chichagof Island, Alaska

rounded us. We repiled gear on seat cushions and life jackets and started jamming things in faster. By the time the job was done, we were a hundred yards from shore in a foot of water.

Somehow we got aboard. Gear was so tightly packed around my seat that I could not wedge myself in far enough to touch bottom. My partner, Dave, had to pile thirty pounds of gear on his legs after getting in. But we were afloat and eager to get going, which we did, paddles clashing.

The afternoon's rain began then, and continued doggedly for the remainder of the day. Dave discovered that his 60-40 cloth parka repelled none of it, and spent the rest of the trip wrapped in a ripped plastic poncho, purchased for $1.19 and tied about him with lengths of rope found on the beach.

Loading Up

Loading kayaks is an art—making the many-shaped items of equipment and duffel conform to your boat's rigid cavities, yet distributing the weight properly and having what you want available in the cockpit. Fitting all your gear in

All of this really does fit in the kayak!

may seem hopeless at first (especially in folding boats that have far less room). On our Sitka trip, loading became faster and easier with each successive day. We gained room not only by using up supplies, but also by learning to pack it more effectively.

With rigid fiberglass boats, loading can be done on the beach or even in camp and the loaded boat carried to the water. Folding boats are more delicate. It is best not to carry them loaded. If you do, support the hull evenly. (Four people with carrying straps under the hull are really needed.) Loading where there is any wave action over an abrasive bottom (especially barnacles) is very hard on fabric hulls. I always try to load my Folbots in shallow water or just above the water on sandy beaches.

The loaded boat should sit evenly in the water with no list to either side and slightly heavier in the stern. How much more weight you will need to the rear depends on your boat and how it performs. If steering is difficult, try shifting more weight toward the stern. One of the best ways to keep the bow light is by packing low-density items like sleeping bags and pads up there.

Unfortunately, the more you consolidate things in big bags before loading, the harder and less efficiently they will load. You can get more mileage out of filling the boat item by item, selecting just the right nook for each one. Somehow a compromise has to be struck, such that most gear is snugly stowed in waterproof bags, with smaller items that can stand wetting (coffeepot, cook set, fuel and water bottles, diving gear, etc.) packed in the interstices. Carry a large, open-topped tote bag to hold all the loose things while you load and unload.

KAYAK LOADING PLAN KEY
INSIDE

1. Sleeping pad
2. Sleeping bag; tarp underneath
3. Shotgun in case
4. Wet suit and diving gear
5. Pack with lunch, compass, and survival gear
6. Camera bag
7. Sponge under seat
8. Bilge pump secured to side; water bottle underneath
9. Collapsible water jug, accessible for use in self-rescue system. Diving weight belt underneath; spare charts against bulkhead behind
10. Foul-weather jacket and pants
11. Fishing gear
12. Food duffel bag
13. Empty tote bag
14. Tent
15. Clothing and miscellaneous duffel bag
16. Cook set, coffeepot to right
17. First-aid kit, fuel, and water bottles aft

ON DECK

1. Mast for sail
2. Four-inch screw-out hatch
3. Bowline tucked under shock cord
4. Emergency paddle
5. Sail rolled on cross-spar
6. Chart case
7. Rudder cocking line and jamb-cleat
8. Sea anchor under shock cord
9. Rudder steering cables

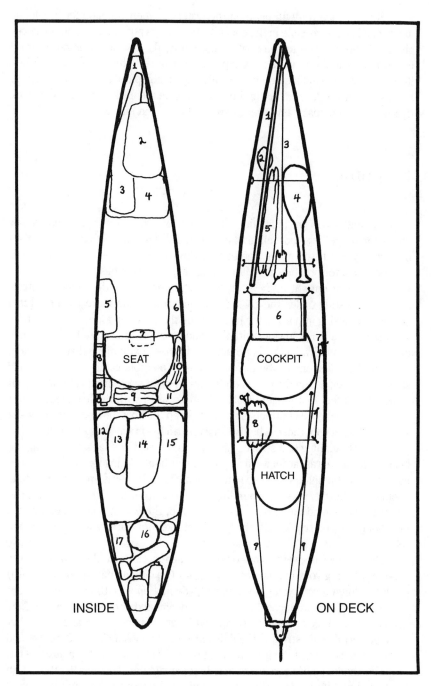

The author's fiberglass K-1 loaded for a month-long trip

All the things you will need on the water or when you stop for breaks or lunch should be accessible in the cockpit. As much as possible, gear in the cockpit should be secured to the boat. Bilge pump, flares, and other rarely used emergency supplies can be duct-taped into an out-of-the-way corner. Other items to have on hand include foul-weather gear, compass, camera, binoculars, snacks, water bottle, and charts. I usually keep in the cockpit a small day pack that holds my compass, emergency survival gear, and lunch.

Paddling

Paddling styles are highly individualized, as there are few absolute dos or don'ts for propelling yourself across salt water. The suggestions here reflect my own style, but you might find them awkward or inefficient. Whatever feels comfortable after practice and after a long haul is what is best for you.

I like to sit upright in the seat, feet lightly braced on the rudder controls and knees resting under the cockpit coaming for a little more balance. Firm contact forward is important for transferring the paddling force to the boat.

Strokes are long and slow, with the paddle never tilting more than forty-five degrees horizontally. There is no need to immerse any more than the blade. Keeping the other end of the paddle as low as possible catches less wind and keeps you drier, as the drip rings on the upper shaft shed their water as far out as possible. I feel that longer strokes do more work with the least extraneous motion and give more continuous power to keep the boat moving, but many sea kayakers (especially those who use shorter paddles) take shorter strokes.

At the beginning of a stroke, I straighten the arm on that side, putting the blade in the water as far forward as possible without leaning forward. My other hand is, at that point, quite close in front of my face. Power is applied lightly and evenly with both arms—one bending while the other straightens—until the blade is well behind me, where it comes out of the water. Sometimes I rotate my shoulders and trunk with the paddle strokes for variety and a bit of arm relief.

The distance between hands on the paddle functions similarly to gears on a bicycle. Moving your hands closer together (no closer than shoulder width) produces "high gear"; you get the most blade motion with the least movement of your arms. This produces the best speed downwind or on smooth water. Low gear, used for slogging upwind, occurs with hands farther apart and slower but more powerful blade strokes. Hand distance really does make a difference, and I often am surprised at the improvement when I remind myself to adjust it a bit.

The paddle blades can be *feathered,* set at right angles to each other. With feathered paddle blades, the upper blade is horizontal, causing less wind resistance than does a vertical blade. When paddling to windward, feathering can make a real difference. Also, feathered paddling is considered more efficient because it takes advantage of the body's rotation during the paddling motion. But feathering can cause tendinitis because of the twisting motion of each stroke. I have had elbow pain after long paddle trips with feathered blades and now only feather them for windward work.

Paddling with feathered blades involves a *control* hand that holds the shaft firmly, twisting it by wrist action to get the proper angle for each stroke. The other hand shifts its grip on the paddle about ninety degrees with each stroke. Use whichever hand suits you for control. That one gets the tendinitis; the other, blisters. Try to learn to switch control hands, though that never has been easy for me.

Some people have trouble changing back and forth between feathered and unfeathered blades. Also, the bracing strokes discussed next can produce disastrous results if the blade turns out to be at a different angle from what you had expected. It is wise to practice all your bracing and rolls with a feathered paddle, assuming that will be the best setting for conditions most likely to require those maneuvers. Feather the paddle whenever you come into a situation where bracing might be required (rips, eddies, or rough water).

Bracing Strokes

There are two bracing strokes made with the paddle that greatly enhance your stability and can avert a capsize.

The low brace should be practiced by every kayaker until it is a reflex. This response is used to counter a loss of balance to one side or the other. You simply slap the paddle blade flat on the water and push down to restore your balance. With practice, the low brace can be used to right yourself even when you have gone so far over that a shoulder is in the water.

The sculling brace (or high brace) provides a long-term platform of stability. You lean to the side, sweeping the paddle through the water just below the surface with the blade angled so that it is forced upward. The paddle is then swept backward with the blade angled so that it will again rise. By sweeping back and forth, the correct blade angles provide lift on which you can put quite a bit of weight. By leaning slightly in that direction and relying on the upward pressure of the paddle, you reduce the risk of a capsize in the other direction.

The sculling brace is useful in big, side-on waves, which would tend to tip you away from them as they hit. Sculling into them helps prevent that. The sculling brace also is useful when your boat is rendered unstable by swamping or while taking a passenger from a swamped kayak onto your rear deck. In the latter case, a person climbing aboard causes unexpected balance shifts to either side. Sculling while he or she gets settled belly-down across your deck is the best way to provide a firm platform until you are ready to paddle off.

There are numerous other strokes and braces mainly used in white water but sometimes useful on the ocean. They are covered in detail in kayaking manuals. Likewise for the complex and somewhat difficult Eskimo roll; I refer the reader to expert advice in manuals or sea kayaking classes.

Paddling in Wind and Rough Water

A long pull into a stiff headwind can be backbreaking, yet upwind travel often is necessary. Both paddlers in a double will get wet, the forward person from waves breaking on the bow and the rear one from spray off forward's paddle (especially a feathered one). Both wind resistance and the force of waves hitting the bow constantly impede forward motion. A long crossing into a headwind merits careful consideration, since covering the distance will take longer than usual and resting means losing ground.

Staying very close to shore while going upwind may be helpful since winds tend to be weaker there. Also, you can see your progress more easily than you can farther out. Paddling strokes should be slow but firm. Keeping steady pressure on the blade is more important than pushing really hard. If there are intermittent gusts, do not wear yourself out fighting them. Ease up on the strength of the stroke during each gust, resting slightly while maintaining just enough pressure to keep the boat moving forward.

In crosswinds, paddling is easier but tricky. Winds pull at the raised blade. (Unfeathered blades work better.) Wave height changes and rolling of the boat mean you will have to watch when and where you dip your blades. Choppy seas coming from the side easily slop over the decks of most kayaks, which is no problem if you have a thoroughly watertight, strong spray cover.

Going downwind can be delightful. It is a good time to raise your paddle in the air to catch the breeze or to put up your sail and relax (as long as the waves behind are not too big). On the last day of a journey in the Queen Charlottes, two of us in a double kayak covered the last ten miles with a thirty-knot tail wind, clocking ourselves at almost six knots with a combination of paddle and sail. It was truly exhilarating and deceptively easy. The wind seemed much lighter because of our downwind progress. By careful control of the rudder, I was able to keep the boat going straight downwind, though it tried to veer to one side or the other as the bow buried in each wave. The size of the waves did not worry me until one broke clear over the stern and struck me in the back. Fortunately, at that point we rounded the bar at Sandspit and entered quiet water.

If you are sailing and steering downwind with your rudder, keep your paddle handy to prevent a broach (turning sideways to the waves). If the boat starts to veer sideways as it surfs down a wave, the rudder may not be sufficient to counteract the turn, but a properly timed paddle stroke can prevent it. If you end up broached to waves, be sure to lean and brace into the waves, not away from them. Part of the cause of broaching is going too fast on the downwind side of a wave, with the result that the skidding boat loses directional stability. Drop your sail and slow down.

Coastal Route Selection

Unless the route you have selected follows unbroken and unprotected coastline, the textures of shoreline and offshore features can do a lot to ease your passage. Close to shore, the kayak comes into its own, making use of tiny reefs, rocks, and even kelp for shelter. Here you can take passages far too small and shallow for other boats and haul out for refuge when other boats must ride it out at anchor.

One learns from experience about what shelter or exposure results from particular features under varying weather conditions. More important, you can learn to visualize them from studying your chart. Considered in combination with the day's likely weather, the chart can help you anticipate the challenges of a route. The examples following are based on actual places in northern British Columbia and Southeast Alaska, modified to give textbook illustrations of some of the common situations that you can predict by using charts.

Chart I demonstrates some basic features of nautical charts. (Complete keys to chart symbols are found in U.S. and Canadian charts Number 1.) The chart illustration (of which the lower right-hand corner is shown) is of a most useful scale, 1:40,000. But this scale in itself does not help much in determining distances. Though many charts include a scale, the easiest way to check distances is to look at the edges of the chart. You will find degrees and minutes of latitude on the north–south edges and of longitude on the east–west edges. The smallest gradations (minutes) correspond to one nautical mile (1.15 statute miles) on the latitude edges only. (Increments shown on the longitude edge are much smaller in the higher latitudes because the Mercator projection used in nautical charts converges longitude measurements toward the North Pole.) In latitude, there are sixty nautical miles (or minutes) between degrees. In the illustration, the island is at fifty-seven degrees, five minutes north latitude. The distance from top to bottom of the illustration is about two minutes, or two nautical miles.

Water depths are shown in fathoms (six feet). Depths of less than ten fathoms usually are shaded light blue, and there is usually another contour line denoting areas less than five fathoms deep. In these shallow areas, a smaller number next to the fathom sounding indicates the additional depth in feet (such

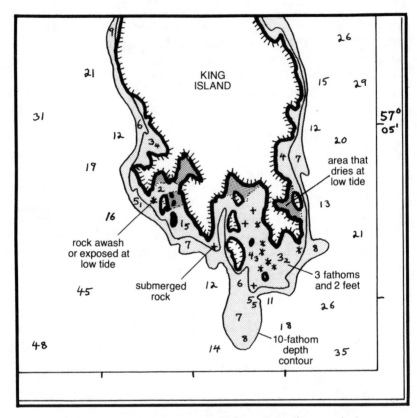

Chart I. Typical features on U.S. or Canadian nautical charts. The light shaded area is water less than ten fathoms deep; the dark shaded areas dry at low tide.

as one fathom and three feet, a total of nine feet at mean low tide). Areas that dry at low tide are shaded brown or olive drab. Rocks that uncover at low tide are shown in brown, or, if small, as an asterisk with a number indicating the height when exposed. Rocks that remain submerged show as a cross.

Though charts are amazingly accurate, they do include inaccuracies and sometimes treat features in generalized ways, especially on smaller-scale charts. After all, they were designed to help larger craft keep off the rocks, not to go behind, between, and even over them, as kayakers often do. So it is not surprising that the inner margins between sea and shore are treated with less accuracy than what lies farther offshore, such as the thirty-fathom depth contour scrutinized by the commercial salmon troller (to whom accurately represented bottom features mean the difference between catching fish and losing expensive gear). Charts, then, are guides to what to expect, but actuality may be somewhat different.

In Chart II, Canoe Pass looks like a protected, interesting route for a kayak.

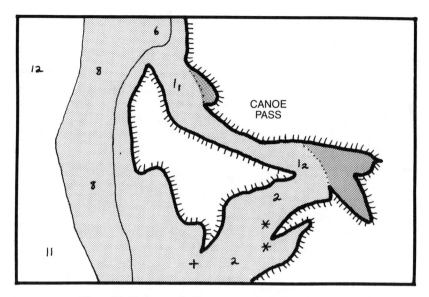

Chart II. Narrow, shallow passages such as this one may not have enough water at low tide, even though the chart suggests it does!

The chart shows that it should be open, even at low tide. But I found that it is not open; the passage is dry for a distance on all but the highest tides. Perhaps at one time the passage was open, but storm-deposited sand or debris filled it during one winter season; another such storm could some day open it again. But since the passage is useless for most navigation, its status is unlikely to be updated regularly.

In some areas of Southeast Alaska, receding glaciers have resulted in postglacial rebound—the land rising at a rate that renders charts of shallow areas inaccurate. This is especially true around Glacier Bay's Beardslee Islands, which are rising at the rate of a foot every eight years.

Currents, Rips, Overfalls, and Whirlpools

The effects of tides, sometimes amplified by winds, may be felt wherever water is moving and constricted by land masses. Those effects range from dangerous to bothersome, interesting, or fun. They may change position, disappear, and reappear.

Rips are steep, closely spaced waves caused by the collision of water moving at different speeds or even in opposite directions, or by water moving over shallows. Rips can overturn a fast-moving boat or upset a narrow-beamed kayak. In narrow passages, fast-moving streams called tidal jets may have many of the characteristics of white-water rivers, including standing waves, strong eddies, boils, and holes. Eddylines (where currents moving at different speeds or directions meet) can produce strong hydraulic effects. The level of one stream can be a foot or more higher than that next to it, an overfall. Whirlpools sometimes occur where the jet current rubs against the slower or backward moving eddies on each side, often disappearing and reappearing. They can be extremely dangerous to small craft, especially at Dent Rapids behind Vancouver Island. (See *Alaska* magazine, July 1977, for an account of two canoes caught in those whirlpools.)

One problem condition for kayakers is caused by contrary winds and tides. When the tide runs against the wind, the result is often steep, inordinately large waves—truly unpleasant for kayaking. Johnstone Strait behind Vancouver Island is well known for this condition.

In Chart III, the mouth of Koyah Pass may present serious problems in entering or exiting the pass, or in crossing its mouth. Since the pass drains a vast internal waterway, the tides in the narrows can run up to eight knots on the ebb or flow. The ebb would be most important to you in your kayak, as you could be carried a considerable distance out to sea before being able to get out of the ebb stream. Rips, whirlpools, and overfalls all could be expected, especially on the shallower south side. If a westerly or southwesterly wind were blowing against the ebb flow, very rough water could compound the problem.

Obviously, the best solution for crossing or entering the pass is to enter on the slack between tides; second best would be to use the flood tide. If you must enter the pass on the ebb tide from the south side, try it very close to the shoreline. There is likely to be a system of eddies just before and after the south point, perhaps even back eddies moving toward the mouth. At the point, you will be on your own, with the full force of the jet current against you. There will be a strong eddyline as you leave the relatively still waters of the eddies and enter the fast ebb jet. Try to cross it as obliquely as possible, allowing the bow of your boat to knife into the jet stream as parallel as possible to its flow. If you cross the line at right angles, you could be forced out into the jet, or end up pointed away from where you want to go. Balance and brace to the downstream side, as the jet stream will tend to unbalance you toward the upstream side as you enter it.

Once in the jet stream at the mouth, the only alternative is to paddle hard, staying as near as possible to the shore (where the current may be slower), and try to gain ground. In this case, you will not have far to go, as there are eddies just behind the south point. Rudder into them as soon as possible to rest and continue in the same fashion.

If you must cross on the ebb, it would be better to cross about two miles

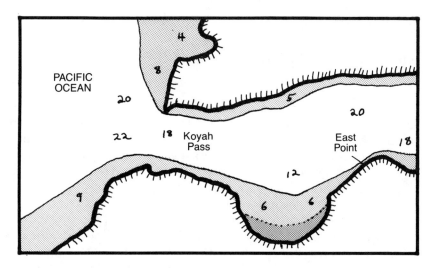

*Chart III. Narrow passages that constrict large
volumes of tidal flows can have dangerous rips, whirlpools, and
fast currents. Approach them carefully.*

inside at East Point. Since it is wider there and as deep as at the mouth (note the fathom soundings), the current will be slower. Also, if you cannot hold your own in the current there, you would have time to retreat to the eddies on the south side before being swept through the mouth into the worst of the turbulence.

Such a crossing calls for *ferrying* technique — paddling upstream and across at an angle that will get you to the opposite shore. The technique is widely used by kayakers and canoeists in rivers. In the ocean, ferrying requires a bit more calculation because crossings usually are much longer than on rivers. If the current is strong, you may have to give it all you have for a fairly long time to make it, so gauge the angle of your boat to cross as quickly as possible without losing more ground than you wish.

To find the right angle, head into the stream, paddling upstream and across. Take a *range* to keep tabs on how you are doing by picking two points on the opposite shore, one behind the other, such as a boulder on shore and a tree behind, adjusting your angle of crossing to keep the two points aligned with each other. This allows you to cross as fast as possible while maintaining sufficient upstream speed. On a long crossing, this ferrying angle can make a big difference in energy output. Keeping an eye on your reference points will enable you to maintain the best angle as you cross, adjusting as you encounter faster or slower currents.

Once across, ease down toward the mouth on the north shore, using the eddies to get around the north point and staying out of the jet current as much as possible.

Finding Shelter
on Exposed Shoreline

There are many places on the outer coast where you have no choice but to be exposed to the open Pacific. On a calm day, the rolling swells can be soothingly pleasant (unless you are prone to seasickness). A moderate chop added by the wind makes the open ocean more uncomfortable and slows progress. Winds are apt to be stronger and seas rougher than on inland waterways. Thus, in all but the best of conditions, exploiting what shelter the shoreline does offer becomes important.

On the outer coast, capes, points, or headlands will usually give you the most challenging paddling. If you are rounding a major cape that defines the end of a large land mass, you can expect stronger winds and more turbulent seas than on either side of it. Onshore wind flows are diverted by the land mass and speed up as they are funneled past the cape. The same thing happens with tidal currents, sometimes producing rips off the cape. The result may be an untenable situation, though the surrounding seas on the approaches are docile. One highly experienced British sea kayaker on a solo expedition had to make two attempts on rounding Cape Ommaney at the south tip of Baranof Island. His comment on the experience: "It gave me religion."

If you need to round a cape under marginal conditions, treat it like a final assault on a mountain peak. Camp as close to it as you can, or try to find a place to get out to rest just before rounding the cape. A few minutes on dry land can do a lot to restore strength and to keep seasickness under control. Use the time to scout the route from ashore, if possible. Some capes or points end abruptly; you have few alternatives other than to find the smoothest water offshore and to get around as fast as possible. Others have offshore features that can provide shelter or give you problems.

In Chart IV, Point Fury presents common challenges. The southerly extension of the point presents a solid cliff face to the oncoming swells. The swells strike the cliff (at an angle if the swells are westerly) and are reflected back. The result is a very choppy area of confused sea within a hundred yards of the sea cliff, with waves running counter to and colliding with each other, making paddling laborious and uncomfortable. Head offshore a few hundred yards from such unbroken sections of coastline, since the wave reflections diminish with distance.

The chart suggests that the northern part of Point Fury offers safer, smoother passage, plus places in which to rest or even to get out and stretch. The whole area is shallow, which may cause steeper waves (due to friction of the wave cycle on the sea bottom) or breakers (due to submerged rocks). On the other hand, the shallows also provide sheltering reefs and kelp beds.

A few words about breakers: a wave or swell breaks when it encounters

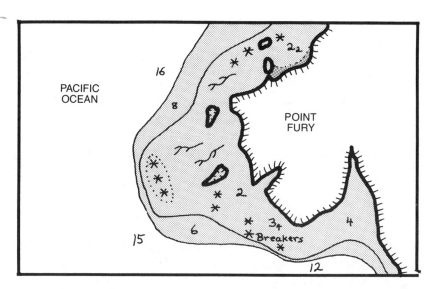

Chart IV. Shallows on a point on the open Pacific can be both a hazard (due to breakers) and a blessing (rocks and kelp dissipate the ocean swells, providing smoother water in their lee).

shallows, such as a reef or a sandbar. However, if there is deep water shoreward from the shallows, the wave will revert to its previous, rounded shape.

Periodically, swells join together to form an extralarge wave, though the interval between such big waves is not always the same. These sequences are called *sets*. The combination of moderate and big waves produces intermittent breakers at some spots, with breaking only on the big ones—an unpleasant surprise for you if you are in the wrong place when a large wave comes along. Previewing shallow areas on the chart can alert you to such hazards. West of Point Fury are many reefs and rocks, roughly located by the asterisk symbols for rocks and shoals awash at low tide. Depending on the swell size, tide height, and wind, some of these may break continuously, or only occasionally. When you are about to enter an area the chart indicates as being likely to have breakers, stop a hundred yards away and watch the wave sets. Look for the big waves. Where do they break? How often do they arrive? If you spot such irregularly breaking areas, you will have to keep track of them as best you can and stay clear, noting their location in relation to more consistent bearing points, such as reefs.

Hazards such as these simultaneously mean shelter. Offshore breakers greatly decrease the size of swells in the lee of the place where they break. It is difficult to predict from the chart how much shelter is likely inshore from the reefs west of Point Fury, but there will be some. I would probably pass just inshore of the four reef indications and the islet, expecting some shelter from westerly swells for some distance in good to moderate weather. (In rougher weather, extensive breakers would make this a bad place to be, as with the point in general.)

You often can find some shelter if your chart shows the Y shapes indicating kelp. Lying on the surface, these seaweed beds tend to flatten the waves and reduce choppiness due to wind. Kelp beds usually indicate water too deep for swells to break, as kelp grows in water fifty to one hundred feet deep. (However, at low tide, the long fronds may stream over shallow rocks where waves break.) If the water is extremely choppy with reflected wave backlash off rocks, steering through kelp beds may be the easier route. I have never found such beds to be impassable, although they do require harder paddling.

Entering or exiting narrow passages leading into open ocean can be especially dangerous. There are quite a few of these used by small boats on the North Coast; some are harmless in calm conditions but perilous in other weather. Chart V shows such an entrance, based on a real place. The chart itself indicates potential for trouble—the rock lying just outside the tiny passage could indicate a clear route behind (east of) it, or breakers all the way across. You will not know for sure until you get there. Again, stop and check it out, watching for intermittent breaking on the big waves. The entire entrance may be quite shallow, resulting in breakers that sweep completely across, as they were when we encountered this particular place. The entire entrance broke on the big waves, but was relatively calm in between. We waited, estimating the frequency of the big waves, and ran for it just after one of them. We were exposed to the breaking area for almost a minute, gambling that we were unlikely to encounter a big swell during that time. It was a calculated risk I would not care to take again.

When in doubt, wait. Waiting for a higher tide level decreases the chances of breakers (if the wind stays constant), just as waiting for the usual calm of late afternoon may resolve a wind problem. Meanwhile, get out, climb up on a rock, and scout the situation. From this height, you may have a better perspective; you may decide that it looks easier than you thought, or that it surely is suicidal. Conditions may improve or deteriorate while you wait. Minimizing the chance of a lethal mistake can make hesitation well worthwhile.

Long Crossings

Crossing open water is the test of an ocean kayaker's preparedness and judgment. That is where he is most vulnerable to nasty weather and where rough-water survival methods and the paddler's wherewithal are most likely to be put to the test. Most crossings are simply long, tedious stretches of continuous paddling with little apparent progress except at the beginning and end. For me, it is always a relief to put such a crossing behind, regardless of the weather.

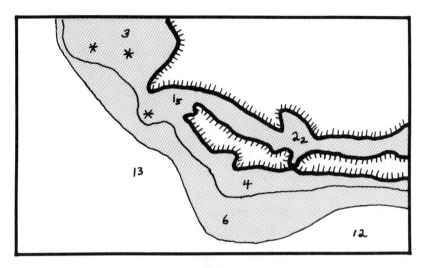

*Chart V. The margin between protected water and the open sea
is often the most dangerous. Here, the submerged rock off the
entrance to this tiny passage causes breaking conditions
on bigger waves—not a good place to linger.*

A crossing should be undertaken only after considering how long it will take and the likelihood of favorable weather throughout. If no more than three miles are involved, the crossing can be made in an hour or less, and you will never be more than a half-hour from either shore. That is a good safety margin in case the weather takes a turn for the worse after you set out. On a crossing of more than six miles, you will be at least an hour from shore at midpoint, and a lot can happen to the weather in that time. Consult the current table carefully to be sure the tide will be in your favor as much as possible.

Try to make long crossings early in the morning. If the sea is calm after dawn, generally (but not always) it will stay that way until late morning. If you have had a still, overcast day all morning and into the afternoon, it may stay that way through the rest of the day. But these rules are fallible; fronts and squalls come and go. If you are carrying a VHF radio receiver, use it to get the big picture from the marine forecast, including current status reports from weather reporting stations around your area.

Make sure you are prepared for the worst before you head out. If you carry a wet suit, this is one time to wear it. Are the bilge pump and other elements of your self-rescue system accessible? If you have a sea anchor, it should be on deck, ready for deployment. Be sure your compass is handy in case of fog. Fill at least one water bottle, stashing it and some high-energy snacks in the cockpit.

During the crossing, keep up a steady pace to finish as quickly as possible. In a double boat, you may want to take turns resting in order to keep moving. While making a crossing, I keep a running check on my surroundings to assess progress and drift. I take a variety of ranges—checking one feature against another behind it—to locate my position on the chart. Ranges ahead and behind my course are used periodically to check for drift due to current or wind. I have also discovered some distance yardsticks; for instance, I can distinguish the individual trees in a mountainside forest from about two miles away. At one mile, I can pick out their various branches.

Compass Navigation

All nautical charts include compass roses, as shown in the following photograph, which indicate true north bearings on the outer circle and magnetic

Working out and steering a course. Use the chart's compass rose to select it and set the compass as described in the text. Here, a course of sixty degrees is being steered, with the kayak's bow toward the top of the photograph.

bearings on the inner circle. Since your compass reads magnetic bearings, the inner circle is what you will use to navigate from a chart. The working out of a course is best done ashore, where you can unfold your chart to include a compass rose. Lay a straightedge along the course you will want to travel on the chart and mentally transfer a parallel line to the nearest compass rose to determine your course. Few kayakers carry the adjustable, parallel rules that navigators use for this job, so practice making the transfer by eye. You should be able to do it with sufficient accuracy for courses of ten miles or less, unless you must locate a very small destination point.

Steering a course with a hand compass is more involved than with a permanently installed one. Lay the compass out flat with the mirror top open and turn the bezel (the movable ring around the face) until the desired course is aligned with the compass case's longer edge, and lay it in the chart case with this edge aligned fore and aft. The desired course is steered by keeping the north-pointing needle aligned with the arrow on the compass face.

One word of caution: metallic equipment in your boat can cause any compass to read improperly. Keep such items away from your compass and check for distortion by taking a bearing to a known and visible point, comparing it to what it should be on the chart. (This exercise should be done anyway to ensure that you are doing the procedures correctly before you have to rely on them in foggy weather.)

Riding Out Heavy Weather

I always have been able to finish a crossing and get out of the water before conditions got too bad to keep going. But there could come a time when there is no choice but to devote all of your attention to just staying afloat. As remote as the occasion must seem, be prepared for it. Weather can change quickly in the summer on the North Coast. Fortunately, squalls or gales there usually do not last too long.

Large sea anchors (*sea chutes* or *drogues)* are useful for riding out rough weather by keeping the bow pointed into the wind. John Dowd reports that smaller ones will not stop backward drift, and that since the boat then yaws back and forth as it drifts, broaching to the waves is possible. This can be prevented by a counterforce on the stern, such as another kayak. (The last kayak will still have the problem.) Dowd suggests that a sea anchor be used with a buoy and at least one hundred feet of line to ensure that the bow is never pulled down by the submerged sea anchor as big waves roll by.

If you are going to sit it out behind a sea anchor, cock your rudder and squirm down low in the cockpit. Keep your paddle ready to use until you are convinced that the boat is riding safely without the need for bracing or corrective strokes. Even then, keep the paddle assembled and on deck, preferably held fore and aft under your arm.

In lieu of trying to stay bow-to-the-wind, some kayakers find lying broadside to the waves a satisfactory way to ride out heavy weather. Because they are light, kayaks tend to ride up and over most big waves, unlike larger craft that take the waves over the deck. The best way to preserve your balance is by bracing upwind into waves. The kayak's downwind movement and downward slide on the faces of waves will give lift to the paddle blades in the water. As long as the spray skirt keeps out all but the drips and is strong enough to resist water breaking over the deck, a kayak should be able to last out short squalls this way.

Landings

The kayak's ability to get ashore almost anywhere is its distinguishing feature. I usually limit my landings to reasonably hospitable places. The so-called seal landing—in which the kayaker rides a wave onto a rock, leaps out, and grabs the boat—is absurdly hazardous with a loaded boat. Surf is likewise threatening to loaded kayaks. I have little experience in it, having always found calmer ways of getting ashore.

Safe landings can be made in all sorts of places. In protected waters, most any spot will do. On the outer coast, the lee sides of small islands often have a small sand or gravel beach in calm water. Even the outer coast itself can provide safe havens, which can be spied from the chart with some degree of reliability. The first element to study is the foreshore, the intertidal zone shown in brown on both Canadian and U.S. charts. This area dries at low tide and is covered at high tide. In some places, the foreshore will be a half-mile wide; elsewhere, only a few feet. Some small coves dry to their mouths at low tide. If they face on the open ocean, low tide may mean an exposed, rough landing; but high tide may provide a protected landing at the back of the cove (as long as the swells do not produce breakers over the shallow foreshore).

The large-scale charts usually distinguish the composition of the foreshore, even in tiny coves on Canadian charts. U.S. charts say "mud," "sand," "gravel," etc.; Canadian charts use a special symbol for each and apply them more generously than do the U.S. charts. Pay close attention to these, as they tell you what will be scraping against your hull. Sand has the least potential for damage to the hull. Gravel is next (and actually is less abrasive to the skin of a folding boat). At low tide, however, barnacles on larger gravel can severely abrade the hulls of both folding and fiberglass boats. Larger rocks or boulders are common in many small coves facing on the ocean. These make tricky and potentially harmful landing sites unless the water is absolutely calm.

The orientation of a beach or cove in relation to the direction of swell

*The most friendly place to land
your kayak—a sandy beach with no surf*

movement affects how much shelter you will find there. In summer, minuscule coves can provide fair to excellent landing sites if they face away from the predominant westerly swells in fair weather, yet piles of logs and debris show the ravages of winter storms. Keep in mind, though, that an easy landing in good weather in an exposed cove can mean that you will be stuck there if poorer weather comes in while you are ashore.

Open crescent beaches can provide surf-free landings if they curve out to a point at either end. Swells refract around shoreline topography to strike a beach at almost right angles to the direction in which they began the approach but decrease in size as they change direction, so you often can find a fairly calm landing site at either end of the beach near the point, especially if there are offshore rocks or reefs nearby.

If you are going to land in a marginal situation, where there is a strong surge from dissipated swells, sit offshore and watch until you have observed the whole wave set, big ones and small ones. If the pattern of waves seems reliable, go in on the small ones. You can get in quite close, riding back and forth on nonbreaking surges, before you make your move. If there is no offshore surf, loosen your spray cover. Have your bowline ready so you can jump out fast and pull the boat up on the tail end of a surge, before the boat is pulled back out again.

BRIEF STOPS ASHORE

I do not like to spend more than an hour or two at a time in the boat. Things get sore—primarily my rear end and my heels. Besides, I usually see lots of little beaches that lure me to stop to look around and have a snack. If the beach is calm and free of rocks, there is no reason the loaded boat cannot be pulled up a bit and left there, with the bowline secured to a rock, log, or a stake driven into the sand. If the tide is going out, you will have to ease it down to the water a bit, depending on how long you stay.

But if the tide is flooding, the beach is rocky, or surges are coming in, it will be too hard on your kayak to leave it grounded, especially if it is a folding boat. In this case, a Siwash anchorage is called for. That is a means by which your boat can be anchored just offshore and yet be retrieved when you want it. It takes a long bowline, at least fifty feet. At the beginning of your trip, find an old gill net on the beach (where there usually are plenty), and cut out a two-foot-square piece. With light line, tie this up into a pouch to hold a twenty-pound rock.

When you want to use the Siwash anchorage, put a rock in the pouch and tie it to the bowline about ten feet out from the boat. Balance the rock on the kayak's bow, hold on to the end of your bowline, and as you stand on shore, shove the boat out. Let it drift until you are almost out of rope, then yank the rock off the deck. Down goes the rock, and the boat is at anchor. Tie off your end ashore. When you want the kayak back, just pull the whole thing in.

The Siwash anchorage. Tie a rock on the bowline and balance it on the kayak, push the boat out, yank the rock off, and secure the line ashore.

Rescues at Sea

Sea kayakers universally agree that a well-practiced Eskimo roll is the most effective way of recovering from a capsize. If you have a boat that will roll easily, loaded as well as empty, practice rolling back to an upright position until the maneuver comes easily and naturally, even in rough water and in the dark. But if you are a folding-boat owner like me, the difficulty of rolling these beasts means you will have to look to other recovery methods.

Everyone also agrees that it is not sufficient to count on the roll recovery. There will be times when you just cannot manage to get back up, such as when the paddle is not in hand or is tangled in kelp (heaven forbid). At this point, you make a wet exit, leaving you in the water and the boat at least partially full of it.

Rescue in a Swamped Boat

A swamped boat could result from (1) upsetting in calm water due to unbalancing or an unexpected eddyline, or (2) filling or upsetting due to large waves, breakers, or surf. In quieter waters, problems are far fewer. A rescue in rough water is the ultimate challenge. The violence of the weather and water will frustrate rescue actions and lead to feelings of hopelessness or panic. It is hard to say which circumstance is more likely, but you certainly should try to prepare for the latter, remembering that any practicing you do will be a far simpler simulation of what you could have to face.

When there are two or more boats close to shore, it usually is most desirable to use an upright boat to take the spilled kayaker to shore, treat him for hypothermia, and then go back for the swamped boat (if conditions permit). The person in the water can actually be taken aboard the rescuing craft, or can remain in the water, clinging to the deck, as the rescuer tows him to shore.

By far the majority of kayaking time is spent paddling within a half-mile of land, where this rescue procedure usually will be the most prudent course of action. Righting and bailing a swamped boat takes time, and if the dunked paddler remains on the scene without a wet suit, he may well be in advanced stages of hypothermia, incapable of paddling, by the time the boat is ready. Getting a wet paddler to shore as fast as possible is your goal, and it is much more important than salvaging the boat.

The dunked paddler should cling to the stern of the rescuer's boat. And because cold water brings on hypothermia, the passenger should be carried with as much of his body up out of the water as conditions permit. That also will speed the trip to shore by reducing drag.

However, a passenger climbing aboard the stern in rough water can dump the would-be rescuer into the drink. Practice in advance of your trip, preferably with the companions and boats that will be going along. Then you will know how best to carry a passenger and how your boat will handle with the load.

There are situations in which it may be better for the wet person to remain at the scene of the capsize. If you are more than a half mile from shore or if tides and wind make access to shore slow and difficult, it may be faster to bail out the boat and use it to get him ashore. (And, obviously, a person paddling alone will not have the luxury of hitching a ride.)

A boat's design, its load, and internal flotation will determine how it floats when swamped. It must float high enough to keep small waves from washing into the cockpit. Otherwise, bailing is out of the question.

Every boat should carry either a pump or a container for bailing. The job needs to be done fast enough to beat whatever water splashes back in and to empty the boat before the spilled paddler gives out.

Some kayakers feel that a container (such as a two-quart pitcher) is best for bailing. Others feel a high-volume pump works best, especially in a self-rescue.

One way to speed up the bailing process is by limiting the amount of water that can enter the kayak through the cockpit. This can be done by dividing off the boat with bulkheads aft and/or forward of the cockpit.

A second means is the *sea sock*, a cloth bag that goes into the cockpit and fits tightly around the coaming. The kayaker sits in the sea sock and in case of a spill, only the sock fills. Reports of use of the sea sock are very good; swamped boats generally retain a great deal of buoyancy and are easy to bail quickly. John Dowd reports that one woman who had been spilled into the icy Pacific waters literally jumped back into her sock-equipped kayak and then bailed it dry. The socks are a bit of a nuisance to have in the cockpit; rubber knee boots tend to catch in the fabric.

Rescue by an Accompanying Kayak

Lee and Judy Moyer of Pacific Water Sports, in Seattle, have worked out an excellent procedure for using another boat to rescue a capsized kayak. The procedure has been well tested in the waters around Puget Sound.

The Moyers' method entails bailing the boat before reentry, with a rescuing kayaker alongside to help bail and reboard. The bailed-out boat must be

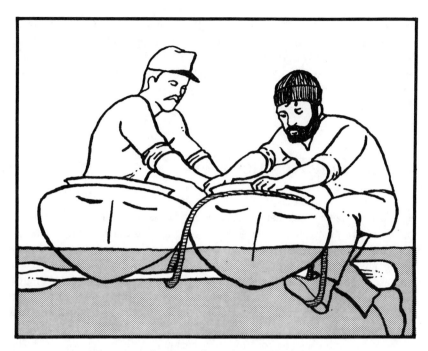

*Recovery after a capsize using another kayak for
assistance. The paddle placed beneath both kayaks helps to
distribute the weight of the reboarding kayaker to both boats.*

steadied during reentry, as most kayaks are extremely unstable during boarding. To ease reentry, a length of nylon webbing is rigged to give the dumped
kayaker a stirrup in which to step. (Fifteen feet of webbing should be plenty to
do the job. The exact length is tailored to the boat's dimensions and varies with
the type of rigging preferred.) The webbing is tied into one big loop, then folded
up and duct-taped out of the way in the cockpit. It can be deployed quickly so
that a loop drops into the water just below the bottom of the boat.

The greatest degree of stability can be attained by using a rigging long
enough to let a loop hang down on both sides of the kayak to be reboarded. A
paddle is inserted into the loop that hangs between the boats and that paddle is
drawn up against the bottom of both kayaks, creating a counterbalance against
the dumped paddler's weight as he steps into the loop at the opposite side of his
kayak. (See accompanying illustration.) Angle the paddle so that it does not
interfere with his reboarding.

A simpler but less stable method uses a shorter loop and eliminates the
paddle beneath the boats. Instead, the webbing loops around the rescued
kayak's coaming. Whichever method is used, the loop should be properly sized
and tied in advance so that the rescue can be effected with speed.

Getting aboard requires a smooth, practiced movement. The rescuer presses down on the cockpit, steadying the swamped boat. On the opposite side, the kayaker in the water faces the cockpit and places the foot toward the bow in the stirrup. He grasps the cockpit toward the front with the forward hand and grasps the far side of the cockpit with the other. The move into the cockpit must be made slowly, balancing against the rescuer's downward pressure on the opposite side of the cockpit.

Kayak Self-Rescues

Some kayakers feel that the Eskimo roll is the only effective self-rescue, but there are many others who feel that a dumped paddler, unaided, can get back into his boat, even in rough water. To be sure, this is the most demanding and lonely task you will ever have, and you are going to have to be very good at it to make it work. Included here are what the optimists about self-rescue agree is the most promising method. Preparations and practice must be done beforehand in warmer water in order for these procedures to work in actual cold-water emergencies.

Getting your capsized boat upright is best done by lying across it, grasping the far gunwale, and lunging backward. Some boats will then remain stable even though filled, particularly the Kleppers, due to their side air bladders. But most will need more stability for reentry. (With a swamped double kayak, one person may be able to hold the bow steady from the water while the other reenters and bails.)

A stabilizing outrigger is far better and vital for a lone person in a single kayak. Matt Broze of Mariner Kayaks in Seattle has developed the Mariner Self-Rescue, described in detail in the user's manual for the Mariner kayak. This method uses a paddle, quickly attached to the deck behind the cockpit, as an outrigger. The attachment must be quite firm to prevent the kayak from rolling toward the outrigger as the paddler climbs into the boat.

Broze suggests attaching the paddle under the shock cords on the deck behind the cockpit (if the kayak is equipped as theirs are). Boats with rounded decks will not provide a very solid attachment, as the elastic cords stretch. Kayaks without shock cords on deck (such as folding boats) will require another means. I use a loop of webbing permanently attached to the deck with an eye-strap. The loop is just big enough to wrap around the paddle shaft with a quick-closure plastic buckle (designed for backpack waistbands), which holds the paddle more steadily than does shock cord. Shock cord will suffice on the opposite side of the deck (away from the outrigger), or you can install a second, similar loop.

A two-gallon collapsible water jug, one-quarter full of water for weight, is used on the end of the paddle to complete the outrigger effect. The jug is

The Mariner Self-Rescue setup, using a collapsible water jug clipped on the end of the paddle

The Mariner Self-Rescue, developed by Matt Broze of Seattle,
uses a paddle and empty water jug as a stabilizing outrigger.

attached to the paddle with a short cord and a snap hook kept on the jug, which is stowed accessibly in the cockpit.

Whether you bail out your boat before reentry or after you get in depends on how well it floats when flooded. Bailing from the water is very awkward and is likely to result in more water flooding in as you reach into the cockpit. You may be incapacitated by hypothermia before you are done.

Some people feel that bailing with a pump from within the cockpit is much more effective and leaves you less prone to exposure—if you can pull it off. The boat must have enough flotation to keep the cockpit well above water once you have reboarded. In choppy water, waves washing in will make it impossible to bail an open cockpit with a container. A high-volume pump (eight gallons per minute) is my preference, as it allows you to close up the spray cover, holding the pump close to your body.

The integral pumps mounted on the decks of the Nordkapp and Umnak Icefloe are lower volume pumps than many portable ones, but they have less water to remove due to the double bulkheads. If you use a hand-held, plunger-type pump, be sure to secure it well in the cockpit (perhaps with duct tape) so you do not lose it when you capsize and can put your hands on it quickly.

What has happened to your paddle all this while? You will never be able to do all these things while hanging onto it (and probably will not have the presence of mind to do so). If you have a paddle-park on deck, stow the paddle there first thing, or put it under the deck's shock cords. But chances are you will lose it, and here is where you will need a spare securely attached to your deck.

Making Yourself at Home

I crawled from my tent into the teeth of a roaring southeaster that promised to last all day. I eased under our tarp pitched against the log pile, where Roger and George administered breakfast. Spooning my Cream of Wheat, I glumly contemplated a day huddling with damp books under the flapping tarp. There would be no traveling today.

Yesterday, a fisherman had mentioned a fish-buying scow in a cove to the north. The chart showed a neck of land separating our slough from Deer Harbor, site of the purported scow.

"What the hell," I decided. "I'll go look it up."

Roger and George would have none of it, preferring more sedentary, relatively dry activities in camp. But they promised to have a chili dinner and a cheesecake (made from a mix) in the works upon my return. I loaded my day pack with survival gear, put on my rain pants (leaving my wool shirt exposed to the rain, which I prefer to sweating inside the foul-weather jacket), picked up my shotgun, and headed down the slough.

At what the chart showed as the closest place to Deer Harbor—a little over a mile away—I took a compass bearing and entered the forest. Dense trees and underbrush kept me from walking far in a straight line, and I had to take new bearings every hundred yards or so. Later, the forest thinned to open muskeg with occasional stands of lodgepole pine, easier going except for large, shallow ponds that had to be circumnavigated. An hour and a half later, after climbing through more thick stands of timber, I hit Deer Harbor right on, to my pleasant surprise.

Twenty or so fishing boats lay at anchor, not a soul to be seen on deck. Close to shore were not one but three scows. The largest, a two-story, barnlike structure, was linked to shore by a precarious gangway of single planks laid end to end and suspended inches over the water. As I made my way along the slippery boards, a listless, dripping German shepherd ambled out to meet me. After giving me a cursory sniff, he turned around and fell in. Oh, well, he seemed to sigh as he scrambled out, what's a little more wet. We both continued to the scow.

Fish-buying scow. This one has a store on the second story.

The store there surpassed my wildest dreams—a miniature grocery of canned and frozen products. Quickly my little pack filled. I paid a surprisingly modest amount and took my leave with a soggy pat for the dog.

My return navigation was not as successful, and I hit our slough the better part of a mile inland. Rounding a corner as I walked along shore toward camp, I stopped in my tracks. A hundred yards ahead, a brown bear sow and three cubs were nosing around in the grass for rodents, unaware of me.

What to do? Far ahead, beyond the bears, I could see the smoke of our campfire. I could detour through the forest, but would chance meeting the bears there if my noisy passage prompted them to take to the woods.

I dropped my pack to gain mobility, chambered a shell in my shotgun, and made myself known by ringing my bear bell, shouting, and waving my arms. Finally, Mama Bear reared to her full height to check me out. Deciding I was just a noisy nuisance, she went back to digging.

This would never do. I redoubled my clamor, explaining my intentions at the top of my voice (mostly to bolster my own confidence). "Hey, Bears, you're in my way! How about heading for home, okay?" After I had continued like this for more than a minute, the sow gave a disgusted shake of her huge head and led the family into the forest. I waited ten minutes, reshouldered my pack, *and scurried past, shouting apologies.*

George and Roger described me as a bedraggled and haunted apparition as I panted into camp, casting nervous glances backward and fingering my gun. I told my tale, but it was forgotten as soon as I opened my pack. A six-pack of beer and two bags of Doritos nested there. Amid the popping of cans and crunching of corn chips, I tossed out the last item—frozen strawberries to top the cheesecake. Ah, wilderness!

Finding a neighborhood grocery just around the corner is far from typical on the North Coast. In some areas, towns and scows are a dime a dozen. Elsewhere, there are stretches of fifty miles or more with absolutely no services. You can count on resupply only in established communities.

For me, a long trip always involves a period of adjustment to living away from civilization's amenities—getting used to sleeping on the ground, reaching a comfortable equilibrium somewhere between clean and grubby, adapting to the isolation from other humans. It may take a week or more of gradual getting in tune with the surroundings as a living environment. This chapter is written to help ease and speed that adjustment.

Campsites

Kayakers do not require much of a place to spend the night. A flat spot for a tent above the high-tide line will do. In some parts of British Columbia or Southeast Alaska, even that is hard to find, as vegetation (especially salal) grows in profusion anywhere above the high-water mark. A jungle of salal, huckleberry, and fallen logs can make it impossible to lie down, much less to set up a tent. In other parts of the coast where there are rocky, convoluted, low-lying islands, finding any place for a layover can be discouraging.

Marine charts can help to identify likely camping spots. Beaches (indicated by finely dotted shoreline on Canadian charts or sometimes by the word *sand* on American ones), especially those in coves backed by valleys, are good prospects. The beach itself may be suitable for camping if spring tides (the extra high, monthly ones) are not expected. Characteristically, the strip of beach just below the vegetation line will stay dry on all but one or two tides a month.

Valley bottoms behind a beach usually support lush plant life. Trees there grow bigger and shade out the underbrush. This means spacious campsites in the forest, where there is likely to be a stream or semipermanent rivulet. If campsites are not turning up elsewhere and you see such an area on your chart, it is worth going out of your way to check it out. Conversely, steeper and higher lands bounded by rocky shore are less likely to have level spots and tend to be

Beach camp in Alaska, complete with fishing boat hulk

poorer growing sites. Particularly on the outer coast of B.C., these environ-
ments are the realm of deep, thick salal and stunted timber—poor camping
sites.

Scanning the shorelines as you paddle along, you can spot likely campsites,
even at a distance. Watch for clumps of big trees, especially cedars. Once, after
scouting for hours along southern Prince of Wales Island, seeking even a medi-
ocre campsite, in the twilight I spotted a grove of particularly tall trees on an
island a mile away. Beneath them was an open carpet of moss and vanilla leaf,
enough room for a platoon to camp.

The chart may point out other desirable campsite features. Note the size of
the intertidal foreshore which dries at low tide (shaded brown on the chart). It
may be easy to haul out at high tide, but it is no fun to leave on the next day's low
tide if you have to lug boat and gear over a quarter-mile of slippery rocks and
seaweed. Waiting for high tide may mean losing good weather as well as time.
Once, in Alaska, we chose a campsite by a mile-long slough that completely
dried at midtide. Morning found us carting our boats and gear over deeply piled
logs in order to launch on a wave-swept outer beach rather than waiting for the
afternoon high tide to flood the slough.

Your chart can give you a preview of coming attractions ashore—access to
good hiking, clamming beaches, views, peaks to climb, rivers to fish, old cannery ruins to explore. Once you get used to reading the charts, you can almost

visualize an area from them.

To select a campsite, follow the fundamental rules presented in your old Scout manual. But there are a few extra things to keep in mind along the wet, stormy outer coast. A camp well sheltered by rocks or forest to the southeast will be much drier and less windy during a storm. More than once, a change in the weather has sent me from a scenic camp in the open to a more mundane, but placid place in the woods.

WATER

Finding water usually is no problem on the rainy coast. But after a week or more of fair and dry weather, some of the smaller streams begin to dry up. The pools they feed may stagnate. Also, a rushing stream may fool you unless you check its source. I once cooked a meal in water from what seemed to be a fine freshwater stream, and sitting down to dine, discovered it had been salt water draining from a slough at low tide. Yuck!

Beware of streams that flood well inland at high tide. You may end up hiking the better part of a mile to get fresh water if dinner will not wait for low tide. From such streams you also may get brackish water at low tide because the stream flows over a long tide flat before getting to you.

Many of the smaller watercourses—rivulets trickling out onto the beaches, pools, or slow-moving streams in the forest—will have a disconcerting brown color. A jug of such water looks like root beer. The color is caused by vegetative decay and leaching organic material and is not harmful as long as the water is not completely stagnant. It may even have a slightly sulfurous odor. But I have used it many times for drinking, cooking, and washing with no ill effects. Be prepared, though, for brownish foods and freshly washed clothes that look like they were not washed at all.

Giardiasis (an intestinal disorder caused by an organism in streams and lakes) has occurred along the North Coast, but instances are rare. (Once it was caused by a trapper throwing carcasses in a stream.) Beaver are prime producers of the cysts that cause it, so avoid streams below beaver ponds or boil the water for at least one minute.

FIREWOOD

Dead or downed wood that you find in the forest usually will be rotten and worthless as firewood. Dead spruce branches on a living tree are often but not always sound. Dead Alaska yellow cedar branches burn very well.

Driftwood is the best bet. Driftwood does not collect along rocky cliff areas or headlands or in confined coves or backwaters. Bays, beaches, and other sheltered areas offer the best scrounging. Driftwood is less plentiful in waterways toward the interior, though beaches facing on large bodies of water often have plenty.

Stashing Your Kayak

I once lost my kayak due to my lack of respect for the spring tide in the Queen Charlotte Islands. I should have known better. It was my second trip to the North Coast, after having spent almost a month on the outer coast of Southeast Alaska the preceding summer. We had pulled into a sandy cove for the evening and were greeted by two local kayakers camping on the way back to their remote home after a shopping trip to town. They told us that there would be a goodly spring tide that night and warned us to stash our boat accordingly.

We thought we did. We put it atop giant logs at the back of the beach, logs that looked as if they had not moved for centuries. The next morning, it was a different beach. The logs all had been rearranged. The massive ones were gone. And so was our boat. After a few heart-stopping moments, I spotted it grounded on a point a quarter mile away. Had it not hung up there, it would have been long gone out to Hecate Strait.

Our paddles, which we had laid across the boat, also were gone. After searching for two hours, paddling with pieces of driftwood, we finally found one of them in a kelp bed. The other we never saw again. A very serviceable paddle was fashioned from a pole and two cedar shakes found on the beach, the whole held together with soft wire and duct tape. We continued on our way penitent and wiser. Now I always stash my boat above the beach or tie it securely. The sea gods reprieved me once, but I doubt they will forgive me again.

The lesson: put your boat above any beach flotsam. If that is impossible, put it as high as you can and tie it to a tree.

The kayak at right is not placed high enough to avoid being carried away by spring tides.

STAYING WARM AND DRY IN CAMP

Any trip of two weeks or more is likely to include at least one day of steady, hard rain and wind. Days like that are best waited out in camp, and might as well be passed in as much comfort as possible.

A tent with a good fly and well-sealed seams is basic. If a tent is not particularly new, carry waterproofed cloth or a piece of plastic to go under the floor, as the ground (especially mossy turf) is like a sodden sponge after a day of rain.

A good-sized tarp (nine by twelve feet or larger) is as essential as a tent. It provides shelter under which to cook, read, and do anything else you do not want to do huddled in a tent on a rainy day. Pitched with a little ingenuity and with the fire nearby, the tarp can turn into a cozy place in the nastiest of weather.

Devise a way to bring the fire as close as possible to the tarp while channeling the smoke away. A fire built at the base of a rock face or cliff (especially where there is a chimneylike indentation or fissure) creates a convection effect that tends to carry the smoke up the face once the rock has warmed. A tarp can be pitched within a foot of the face, and yet the smoke still will be drawn up and away (as long as there is no strong wind). Expect the tarp to sustain occasional burn holes from stray sparks—a reasonable nuisance repairable with duct tape. Lacking a rocky face, similar results can be obtained by constructing a backdrop for the fire from driftwood or old plywood off the beach. These flammable materials must be protected by regulating the fire size or by wetting them down periodically.

Think twice about camping on points, where even in the woods the prevailing wind can eddy, blowing smoke in every direction. In that case, there is nowhere to locate a fire where smoke will not invade your camp.

To start a driftwood fire, some fire starter (either chemical or pieces of dry pitch pine) is vital. Driftwood needs a good bit of initial heat to get going and then requires steady feeding. Tinders found in the forest (twigs, mosses, etc.) seldom work well in very wet weather. Small shards of driftwood found at the high-tide line ignite well over fire starter because this wood dries so quickly. Once a small pile of fragments has gotten well started, larger pieces of beachwood will catch easily and a stoking supply can dry next to the fire. Keep the fire going well, as beachwood does not hold coals very well.

Forest Service Recreation Cabins

The U.S. Forest Service maintains more than one hundred cabins in Southeast Alaska that are available for public use. The cabins may be reserved on a first-come-first-served basis. The fee is $10 per night. Though the majority are located on freshwater lakes, many can be reached by sea kayakers.

Most of the cabins are modern structures, either A-frames or log cabins assembled from prefabricated kits. They usually have wood or oil stoves and wooden bunks and will accommodate from two to eight people. A few of the cabins were built by individuals who held homesite permits. When these leases expired (usually after the occupant had died or moved away), the Forest Service converted the cabins for recreational use. One such huge cabin still bears traces of the original bush homesteader—ancient, rusty tools and spare parts in the workshop, a winch-way for rolling oil drums up from tidewater, and remains of an overgrown garden out back.

You can reserve cabins or take your chances that they will not be in use. Doing the latter is fine, so long as you understand that you will have to get out if someone with a reservation shows up. Many of the cabins are booked up all summer.

You can make reservations in person at agency offices in Alaska or by mail up to six months in advance. From Canada or the lower forty-eight, the best procedure would be to send for a map of the Tongass National Forest and a brochure describing recreation facilities. (See Appendix for address.) Both the map and brochures show the location of cabins, indicate how they can be reached (look for the key word *boat*), and give other specifics. The brochure includes forms for requesting a first-, second- and third-choice cabin, and dates for each. You can get your money back if you cancel out at least ten days before your date of use.

Privately Owned and Abandoned Cabins

One of the highlights of a trip on the remote North Coast is the fortuitous discovery of a habitable old cabin in a cove on a rainy day. There is nothing so fine as spending a dry evening basking by a wood stove instead of huddling in a soggy tent. Cabins and remnants of commercial buildings (such as mines and canneries) dot the coast. Some are occupied intermittently; others, rarely.

Until very recently, there was an unwritten rule that unoccupied cabins were available for anyone to use, especially in emergencies, as long as you replaced the wood you burned and whatever provisions you used, if that was possible. Such universal hospitality is fading due to abuses and the increase in pleasure boating. Locks on the door and "No Trespassing" signs are far more common than they used to be.

Charts offer little help in finding habitable cabins. In fact, I have noted that if a marine chart shows a structure, it is almost certainly no longer there! Many charts originally were surveyed long ago. Many U.S. charts for Southeast

Alaska say "North American datum 1927," when such structures were noted. More recent editions concentrate on updating navigational information, often onshore developments. Hence, old structures remain on the charts and new ones seldom show. Topographic maps are more up to date.

Local word of mouth is the best source of information about usable cabins. In one area, hand-loggers told me of three ancient cabins along my way. I would never have found them otherwise.

Staying Clean

Achieving a comfortable degree of personal cleanliness is a major step toward feeling at home in this wet country for long periods. Otherwise, the latter part of a trip becomes a countdown toward the eventual shower in civilization. There are a number of ways of bathing without much effort or equipment.

Include a hot spring or two in your itinerary. Many are well identified on charts or agency-provided maps; others are lesser known and undeveloped, and you will have the pleasure of discovering them on your own. Some have well-built cabins open for use nearby (at White Sulphur Springs on West Chichagof Island in Alaska, there is a Forest Service public recreation cabin) and even buildings over the pool. Others are more rustic, with rough driftwood bathhouses or just an old bathtub out in the open with plastic pipes positioned to bring hot water from the muddy pool. But whatever the amenities, the morale boost of a hot soak is profound. In the absence of hot springs, tidal pools occasionally make acceptable bathtubs, given sufficient sun to warm the water between tides.

But for convenience—a bath when and where you want it—nothing beats a portable shower. Taking a shower in cool, stormy weather is not as spartan an experience as it might seem. Do some calisthenics to warm yourself up, then strip down and get under the warm water as quickly as you can. You will feel comfortably warm while you shower and afterwards, dress. My shower is a two-gallon, collapsible jug (also used for carrying and storing water in camp and as an outrigger float for my kayak's self-rescue system). Equipped with a rubber shower attachment designed to fit variously sized bathtub spigots and filled with warm water, the jug provides a very satisfying shower. Fill the jug, pour out half of the water, heat it to boiling, and pour it back in. The resulting temperature will be just right. Brace the jug at head height or slightly higher on tree branches or hang it on a tree in a sack made from scraps of gill net (which are easy to find on the beach). Moss or driftwood boards make a nice floor on which to stand. Place the water jug spigot side down, resting the shower head atop the jug. When you are ready to shower, take it in your hand and let gravity

Portable shower using a collapsible water jug

do its thing. Put the shower head back up top while you are sudsing, then bring it back down for the final rinse.

Clean Dry Clothes

Getting clothes serviceably clean is no problem. The challenge lies in getting them dry! For laundry, use two large plastic trash bags. Dig two holes about a foot deep in sand or gravel. Set therein, the bags become washing and rinsing tubs.

Do the washing in the morning, ideally on a sunny day. Wring out your clothes well. Spread them on logs, rocks, or lines strung in the sun, and hope for the best. If the sun lasts the better part of the day, they will probably dry. In nonsunny weather, the humidity will not let clothes dry at all. In fact, dry clothes hung in a tent at night are damp by morning.

Drying clothes by the fire has never worked well for me. I end up with clothes that are soot-stained, smoky-smelling, and still damp after countless hours of tending. But there is another approach that is promising: the hot rock method. I have had some success with it, and suggest further experiments. A rock warmed by the fire can dry a pair of socks or felt boot liners laid atop it. If you have more clothes to dry—say, two pairs of socks, some pants, and a damp sweater—a more elaborate set-up will be needed. At bedtime, roll a number of

Small amounts of clothes can be dried with heated rocks and a cover—in this case, a foul-weather jacket.

hot rocks away from your campfire and under your tarp or other shelter, forming a cluster of them. Then, make a drying rack, a grid of sticks to hold the clothes above the rocks. Spread out the clothes, layering them on as evenly as possible. (If your boots are damp, you might even place them on top, laying them on their sides.) Build a teepee of sticks over everything. Finally, cover the teepee loosely with a ground cover or raincoat. It is important to leave room for air circulation while still retaining the heat in and around your clothes. The rocks hold their heat for a number of hours, and everything will be close to dry by morning.

Food from Land and Sea

The Indians maintained that a person would have to be a fool to starve along the North Coast. Many kinds of food are plentiful and easy to harvest: fish, crabs, and mollusks from the sea, greens and berries from the shore. North Coast residents living outside the major communities glean many of their fresh foodstuffs from their surroundings.

Kayakers can do likewise, but there is a trade-off in the amount of time required to live off the land. Fishing is unpredictable. Dinner may take from seconds to hours to catch. In some places, fish are sparse. Conditions may be wrong. Or, the fish may just refuse to bite. Shellfish almost always are available at lower tides, but eating them involves a risk of poisoning, which I will discuss in a bit. So I have come to regard seafood as a bonus to be enjoyed whenever salmon, cod, abalone, or crab come my way. I carry enough food to do without the seafood, preferring to carry home extra provisions rather than to go hungry.

Sport fishing licenses are required for all saltwater fish in both British Columbia and Alaska. No license is required for taking shellfish other than razor clams in Alaska. British Columbia requires a license for all shellfish. (See Appendix for the addresses of agencies that issue the licenses.)

Fishing

I limit my fishing to rockfish, perch, flounder, ling cod, and other bottom fish; salmon fishing takes a rod and reel (which I find too much hassle to carry) and usually takes more time and concentration than I am willing to commit. (Besides, it is easy to buy a freshly caught salmon from a fishing boat.) In the right place, bottom fish can be hauled in within seconds of dropping the line. Jigging gear is minimal and fits in a pocket: just a bottom-fishing lure, one hundred feet of sixty-pound-test monofilament line, and something on which to wind it.

The best bottom fishing spot is along a rocky shoreline where the bottom drops off steeply. Shallow places (less than thirty feet deep) or sandy bays rarely harbor fish. I go out just far enough to get thirty or forty feet of water. Drop the line until it hits bottom and then reel back about four feet. Raise the

Rockfish caught with the handline above

line up and down three or four feet every five seconds or so. I have found that if I do not get something in the first minute or two, I will not get anything there, so I move on. In that respect, cod-jigging takes little time. If at first I do not succeed, I keep the gear on deck and try it in the most likely spot I see as I paddle along.

I catch more bottom than fish and have lost more than one lure. But the sixty-pound-test line usually allows the lure to be pulled free, even if it means straightening a hook or breaking off a barb. Try paddling around in a circle as you pull on a snagged line; sometimes a different angle will free the lure easily.

The only hazard present in cod (or other bottom fish) is a worm occasionally found in the flesh, curled up in a quarter-inch circle. This parasite—a nematode of genus *Anisakisi*—can infect humans. If you hold fillets up to the light, you can see any worms and cut them out before cooking. And the heat of cooking is likely to kill any worms you might have missed.

Shellfish

Many kinds of clams, mussels, and cockles are found along the North Coast. These shellfish are a much more dependable source of food than are the finny fish. But the shellfish (including oysters, which are not found north of Vancouver Island) come with a lethal price, the possibility of paralytic shellfish poisoning (PSP).

In 1799, one hundred Aleut hunters accompanying the Russian explorer, Alexander Baranof, in Alaska's Peril Straits died after eating contaminated mussels. The place of this tragedy still is known as Poison Cove and Deadman's Reach. Since then, PSP has caused only a few deaths, but many cases of illness occur every year.

PSP is caused by a toxin produced by plankton (specifically, by a dinoflagellate of the genus *Gonyaulax*). Though present year-round in the ocean, these plankton "bloom" or multiply in the warmer months, sometimes producing a visible red tide and killing fish. But not all visible red tides are toxic, and the threat of PSP may be present when there is no visible change in the color of water.

Filter-feeding shellfish (which abalone and crabs are not) concentrate the toxin in their bodies, though they themselves usually are not affected by it. The presence of PSP toxin is neither visible nor easily detected by tests.

Initial symptoms of PSP are tingling of the mouth, face, fingertips, or toes. Paralysis may follow and suffocation can occur if the diaphragm becomes paralyzed. Sustained artificial respiration may keep a victim alive until the toxin wears off, perhaps as much as twenty-four hours later.

Many North Coast residents ignore the hazard of PSP or rely on precautionary folk wisdoms, most of which have little basis in fact and frequently prove unreliable. Some say that you can detect PSP immediately as a slight tingling when a piece of clam is placed on the tongue. Cutting off the black tip of the foot or siphon is supposed to reduce the hazard because that area collects more toxin, but the rest of the body can still harbor a lethal dose. Cockles popularly are regarded as safe from PSP but there is no scientific evidence that they are. Some locals test clams on their cats, which are more sensitive to PSP than are humans. One Petersburg resident tells of feeding a test clam to the cat, which ascended the stairs, then came rolling back down. Out went the clams. Kitty recovered.

Some bivalves pose a greater PSP hazard than others. Mussels concentrate high amounts of the toxin, but dissipate it fairly quickly. Butter clams can retain lethal doses of toxin for up to two years.

The severity of poisoning is related to how many shellfish you eat and their toxin content. In 1981, three Indians on the west coast of Vancouver Island died at a potlatch where prodigious quantities of mussels were consumed. But eating a little and then waiting for effects may not be an effective precaution, since symptoms may not appear for three or four hours. More important, one clam or mussel may contain enough toxin to kill you.

If you do feel some effect from shellfish you have eaten, induce vomiting immediately and use a quick and thorough laxative. These purgatives may not be sufficient, so get to a doctor as soon as possible. Long-term artificial respiration may have to be administered if medical attention is not available.

Unfortunately, there is no way for the layman to test for PSP toxin outside a laboratory. Reliable test kits have not been developed. Health agency tests are made by injecting extract of clam meat into mice and then calculating toxin content from the length of time required to kill the mice. Clams are tested regularly, but since sampling can be done at only a few beaches and since concentrations of the toxin can vary widely (up to 50 percent on one beach), PSP alerts usually are issued for large areas. (British Columbia often posts a warning for the whole coast north of Queen Charlotte Sound.) Even if no alert is in effect, a particular bay still could be hazardous, as toxin concentrations have been known to vary as much as fivefold within a mile.

As a result of all this, I simply stopped eating clams and mussels on the North Coast in the summertime. On my first few trips, I ate them, but sitting around feeling my lips for numbness took all the fun out of it.

ABALONE

Visitors from California usually are surprised by the small size of the North Coast's pinto abalone, which rarely exceeds six inches in length. Small as they may be, these little "abs" are considered more tasty than their southern relatives and are easier to prepare.

Abalone are found on rocks washed by swells from the open Pacific and rarely on the inside waters. The presence of sea urchins is a good indicator of abalone habitat. Abalone feed on algae and hence are not a PSP hazard like the filter-feeding shellfish.

In B.C., only those with shells more than four inches wide can be taken; the minimum size in Southeast Alaska is three and one-half inches wide. Alaska requires a permit for taking abalone. (The permit is free, used to provide the state with harvest data.)

Diving is the best way to collect abs, but you can wade after them on a minus low tide. Often, I have collected them from my kayak on low tides, rolling up my sleeve and reaching down a foot or so.

To prepare abalone, cut the foot away from the shell and remove the viscera at one end of the foot. Slice the foot about a quarter-inch thick, and it will not need any pounding to tenderize. Fry quickly, as for most shellfish, thirty seconds or so on a side. Serve with margarine and perhaps a little soy sauce.

Edible Plants

Edible plants found along the seashore can give you a nice change from dried foods and are a good source of vitamins. There are many edible plants on

Goosetongue

the North Coast. They are best identified with a good field guide (see Appendix); I will just point out a few common ones I use frequently.

Goosetongue (also known as seaside plantain) is ubiquitous. This little plant with spikelike leaves grows profusely on rocks or sand and pebble beaches just below the maximum high-tide line. The younger and more tender leaves can be chopped and eaten raw in a salad, steamed as a vegetable, or mixed into a stew.

Glasswort (also called beach asparagus) is a succulent with many tubular stalks. It grows on mud or sand flats covered by high tides. The stalks are crunchy and a bit salty, very pleasant eaten raw. Cooked, it reminds me of string beans, but better.

There are many plants in the forest that make good salad ingredients— among them chickweed, cleaver, watercress, and young spruce buds. The peeled stalk of a thistle tastes a lot like celery. I often carry a little bottle of vinegar and oil to dress a salad of native plants.

One final but improbable delicacy: stinging nettles. The leaves lose all of their sting when boiled or steamed and make a very nice vegetable dish (especially young leaves). But you will need to use gloves in picking them.

Glasswort, sometimes found in huge quantities on mud flats

Ashore in Bear Country

On my first kayak trip to the North Coast, our party of four prepared to camp after the first day of expeditionary paddling for any of us. We erected our tents in twilight under a massive, dripping spruce.

"Hey, what are these?" someone exclaimed about the line of large, regularly spaced holes next to our camp. He was pounding a tent stake into one of them.

"Beats me," I said, too tired to care.

The next morning, better lighting and renewed curiosity helped us decipher the holes: a brown bear trail. Creatures of habit, the big brownies always step in the same paw prints.

Quickly, we dismembered camp.

Several days later, a companion and I went exploring in a place called Waterfall Cove, a large estuary where bears are likely to be seen. We paddled a half-mile or so upriver to a point where the water is barely deep enough to float our kayak. Standing in the shallows next to our boat, we sighted our first bears,

A young brown bear ignores passerby.

two of them peacefully feeding in grass the better part of a mile away.

Then, less than a hundred yards from us, a young brown bear strolled out of an alder thicket. He looked at us. Our situation was abundantly clear. We could do nothing. Jump in the boat and paddle away? The bear could wade after us and catch up before we had gone a hundred feet, without getting his tummy hairs wet. So, adrenaline surging, we watched. After meandering about for a few moments with no apparent interest in us, he reentered the alder and disappeared. So did we. Pronto.

I was, very frankly, spooked. I did not feel comfortable in the woods for the next few weeks. Then came a day when I was hunting fiddlehead ferns near camp. The little edibles were plentiful, and I soon became absorbed in harvesting the most succulent of them.

Suddenly I froze. I had the feeling that I was being watched. Looking around, I saw nothing. But I realized that I had let down my guard, and an instinctive inner alarm was alerting me to the lapse. The same sudden need to stop and survey my surroundings occurred many times on that trip. I learned the watchfulness of the deer and rabbit, and of our distant ancestors who were not only the hunters, but also the prey.

On the North Coast, bears are a fact of life. The huge, brown bears are a very real threat to safety. Nonetheless, statistics show that the odds of being injured by one are many times less than the chance of being hurt on the nation's highways, and there are many things that can be done to further reduce the odds.

Bears, brown or black, are found all along the North Coast. They are intolerant of each other and rarely are found in the same area. Black bears (*Ursus americanus*), common throughout North America, live on most of the islands of the British Columbia coast, including the Queen Charlottes, and are common on Alaska's Prince of Wales Island. Brown bears (*Ursus arctos*) are found on the mainland and islands of Alaska north of, but not including, Prince of Wales. The greatest concentrations are found on the "ABC" islands: Admiralty, Baranof, and Chichagof. A few brownies have been seen on islands in the vicinity of Petersburg and Wrangell.

Brown bears and grizzlies actually are the same species, but the coastal-dwelling browns attain greater size because of their habitat, which affords abundant food and a longer foraging season than the interior gives to the grizzly. Kodiak bears are a subspecies of brown, genetically isolated on Kodiak Island.

Black bears are the far smaller cousins of the brown/grizzly. Few weigh more than three hundred pounds. They have a more pointed head and nose and lack the distinctive shoulder hump of the brown. Black bears have smaller, sharper front claws, which make them excellent tree-climbers. An adult brown cannot do that easily.

Black bears are not always black. They also come in many shades, ranging from cinnamon through light and dark brown. The sow will bear two or three cubs, which remain with their mother through the first and sometimes the second year.

Along the coast, black bears prefer beaches and nearby grassy spots where they eat herbaceous plants. They also love berries and eat insect larvae and small rodents, when they can catch them.

Compared to the brown bears, black bears are shy and retiring. They usually retreat when confronted by humans. However, the danger of black bears should not be underestimated. They have been known to attack people on the North Coast, and a sow is not reluctant to do so if she feels that her cub is threatened. In popular camping areas, black bears have become accustomed to humans and may be aggressive in raiding camps for food. One such campground is at Bartlett Cove in Glacier Bay, where food must be stored in the bear-proof cache provided and camps kept free of food.

Once, I had set up my camp in a patch of grass by a sandy cove and was sitting on a log in the sun, engrossed in my tide table. Looking up, I saw a black bear ambling down the beach toward me. The wind was in my direction, preventing him from smelling me. The poor eyesight typical of bears prevented his seeing me, my white kayak, my bright blue tent, or the profusion of gear less than a hundred yards from him. Simultaneously I reached for my camera and shotgun, laying the latter close at hand.

The bear walked up to a stream a hundred feet to my left. At its mouth he stopped, disturbed about something. Indecisively, he walked back and forth on a log for a minute or so, close enough that I could hear his feet slapping on the wood. Then I realized his problem. My wet suit was hung out to dry on logs that spanned the stream, and he did not know what to make of the manlike black

Black bear strolling on the beach

shape.

Finally, he decided not to risk an encounter with the black thing and started off up the hillside. It seemed prudent to advise him of my presence for his future reference, so I called, "Bye-bye, bear!" He jumped as if shot, and the diminishing sounds of crashing brush were the last I heard of him.

I would have been wiser to make myself known at the outset. The black bear may attack if confronted at close range and I would have felt very bad had I been forced to shoot him as the consequence of a confrontation I could have prevented.

Had the bear been a brownie, I would not have been a bit relaxed about the encounter. Brown bears often are more than double or triple the size of black bears of the same age. Big ones have been known to weigh three-quarters of a ton and rear nine feet high on their hind legs, though six hundred to one thousand pounds is much more typical of the average adult. Color is usually brown or a dark tan.

Like the black bears, brownies are primarily vegetarians, preferring to forage in grassy areas along the shore and in berry patches of the nearby forest, although they may range into the more barren highlands. Brown bears also are opportunistic carnivores, catching rodents or larger mammals. Male bears will even eat cubs of the same species. During salmon spawning runs, brown bears often congregate in large numbers to gorge themselves on the fish.

Brown bear cubs are born during the sow's midwinter hibernation. They weigh less than a pound at birth, but are much larger by the time they emerge with their mother in early spring. They remain with the sow through two sum-

Brown bear watching for spawning salmon

mers. Sows may give birth to a new litter a year after the first, or may adopt orphaned cubs. So it is not unusual to see a sow with both this year's cubs and yearlings in tow. The average litter size is two to three cubs, but four are not uncommon.

In addition to their size, strength, and speed (brown bears can run at thirty miles an hour for short distances), their aggressiveness is something to be reckoned with. Though brown bears have retreated in every encounter I have had with them (frustrating my efforts to get good photographs), you cannot predict whether they will charge and, if so, whether the charge will be a mere bluff or the prelude to an attack. Maulings and deaths caused by brownies are yearly occurrences in Southeast Alaska. Attacks usually are preceded by posturing and threatening behavior. Repeated "woofing," snapping of the jaws, and bristling of fur along the back are good signs that at least a bluffing charge is imminent. Rearing up on the hind legs is merely a means of getting a better look to determine what you are.

Many unfortunate incidents with brown bears result from the actions of the person involved. It is best to minimize the chance of a close-up confrontation; the bear usually will avoid encountering humans if given ample warning that they are there. Avoid dense forest or alder thickets where you may get close to a bear without either of you knowing the other is in the neighborhood. Make noise to advertise your presence, talking loudly or carrying a noisemaker. Troller bells, which look like little cowbells and are used to signal fish on commercial boats' troll lines, are readily available in marine hardware stores along the North Coast. Wear a bell around your neck so that it rings as you walk.

If you see a brownie, make sure he knows that you are there and what you are. Make noise and wave your arms, anything to suggest that you are a person. Never try to frighten off a brown bear, especially by firing a gun, which has been known to provoke a charge. Since brownies are territorial and concerned with "saving face," give way yourself rather than forcing a bear to leave. If the bear approaches you, climb a sturdy tree (if one is nearby). Never run, as that may provoke pursuit, and the bear probably will win the race. Try to keep your nerve, face the bear, and back off slowly. Keep making noise to establish your identity for a bear that may be approaching out of curiosity. Finally, if you are attacked, play dead, as bears frequently lose interest in something they think has been killed.

In camp, practice "bear etiquette." Never camp next to a salmon stream during spawning, and never camp near obvious bear trails, identified by well-worn footprints in a staggered pattern. Maintain your camp fastidiously. Bears are attracted by food odors and may enter a camp whether you are there or not. Keep your cooking and eating area well away from the place where you sleep, and never take food of any kind into your tent. To be on the safe side, do not sleep in the same clothes you wore to cook or eat, and wash your hands and face after eating. Food should be hung at least twenty feet up in a tree, well away from your sleeping spot. Never leave food in a kayak; bears can destroy it with

*A troller bell worn around your neck warns
bears of your proximity.*

ease. Do not leave dirty dishes lying around. Burn out empty cans and other food containers.

In addition to these precautions, I make my presence known in the vicinity of my camp by walking around the general area. Since bears have such terrible eyesight, it is important to establish yourself by sound and scent whenever you are ashore. Folklore says that urinating around a camp perimeter establishes it as your territory as far as bears are concerned, but the theory is scientifically unproven.

Should you carry a gun in brown bear country? That is a matter of personal preference, as there are points of view on both sides. Most Alaskans maintain that you are crazy not to have a firearm, but other experienced "bush" walkers there disagree. The security of a firearm can lull you into inadequate watchfulness or tempt you to venture into potentially dangerous situations. Then, you had better be able to shoot straight and fast. A wounded bear is very bad news.

Although I am neither a hunter nor a gun fancier, I finally decided to carry a gun as a backup to other precautions in brown bear country. I feel much more secure with it. While avoidance works most of the time (and I still practice it conscientiously), bears are, like people, individuals. There is the ornery one that attacks out of meanness, the sow that defends her cubs against the innocent passerby, the previously wounded bear for whom the mere scent of humans triggers rage.

If you are going to carry a gun for defense against brown bears, it has to be a big one. Most pistols are worth less than nothing, even a .357 magnum. A .44

The author's cut-down twelve-gauge shotgun, an effective
defense against brown bear at close range

magnum pistol (which costs about $250) is one of the most popular weapons carried for defense in Alaska, although some feel even this mammoth handgun lacks sufficient power to stop a thousand-pound bear. I decided against a pistol for two reasons. First, a pistol cannot be carried in or across Canada under any circumstance, (except, of course, on direct flights to Alaska or on the Alaska ferry, which makes no customs stops). Second, I am not confident of my pistol-shooting ability. The .44 magnum is single-action—you have to cock it to shoot. Would I remember to do it?

Rifles and shotguns are bulkier, but more accurate and more powerful. A good choice is the .44 magnum carbine (about $400), which takes pistol ammunition but has greater striking force due to the longer barrel. It is semi-automatic, a mixed blessing as it must be kept immaculately clean to work.

I decided on a pump-action, 12-gauge riot shotgun (about $270) which I cut down to just above the legal length: an eighteen-inch barrel and thirty inches overall. I think that, at close range, a shotgun helps to compensate for less-than-dependable marksmanship. I load the shotgun with two OO buckshot shells, followed by two slugs. For safety, I never carry a round in the chamber. I find the gun easy to carry barrel down in a sheepskin-lined sling.

Being around salt water is very hard on guns. Even though I try to keep drips off it, my gun erupts in new rust daily and must be cleaned as often. There is only one gun preservative that works in that environment, RIG, which stands for Rust Inhibiting Grease. I also put a balloon over the barrel to keep out water and dirt. Some pistols and shotguns are made of plated metal or stainless steel, more expensive but not susceptible to rust.

Guns are allowed for defense in national parks in Alaska, unlike parks in the lower forty-eight. When you enter, Park Service employees will seal your gun with wire so they later can tell if it has been fired.

If you are forced to shoot a brown bear in Alaska, the Department of Fish and Game requires you to turn in the skull and skin (a challenge for you with your Swiss Army knife).

Along the Way

After studying up on the plants and animals of the North Coast, I discovered the obvious—there is just as much to learn about the people who live there and how they earn their livelihoods. Books were less help than the people themselves. I was naive and afraid to ask dumb questions, but found that people appreciated that I did ask and had made an effort to learn a bit in advance. I am still an outsider, but one who has at least a rudimentary knowledge of what their lives are about. The salmon troller appreciates my not calling his boat a "trawler." The Tlingit village administrator I chanced to meet in a Sitka bar spent hours with me, discussing native land claims because I knew a little bit and asked him to tell me more.

Likewise, an understanding of who owns the land along the North Coast heightens my appreciation of what is around me. Though much of the country has the appearance of total wilderness beyond the control of man, it is owned and managed for diverse purposes. Much is changing in public land management, especially in Alaska, and has dramatically affected the lives of the people who live there.

The fishing fleet, the coastal Indian population, and the public forest lands are among the most important and unique elements of this region. I hope that what I am able to describe in this chapter will give the kayaker who paddles this coastline a brief introduction to what characterizes life on the North Coast.

The Fishing Fleet

Commercial fishing craft will be your constant companions almost anywhere on the North Coast. There is a lot of reassurance in seeing a few trollers working nearby as you round an outer coast headland in ominous weather. Those fishermen are a good source of weather reports and may be willing to relay messages for you via their VHF radio. Many fishermen are intrigued with kayaks and want to know all about them. Their respect for kayakers is enhanced if you in return show some knowledge of and interest in their boats and gear and what they do.

Commercial fishermen are the survivors of a vanishing breed of independent entrepreneurs. Their boats are their livelihoods as well as their homes during the season (and, for some, almost year-round). Fishermen value their independent life-style and rankle at the efforts of government agencies to regulate them.

A large number of the fishermen who spend summers working Canadian and Alaskan waters are not residents of the area. At the end of the season they head south to Puget Sound, where they spend their winters at other jobs or working on their boats. Most head north in May or June and return home by mid-September or early October.

There are at least a half-dozen kinds of fishing boats that kayakers will see on the North Coast. The two that cause the most confusion for the nonfishing public are trawlers and trollers. You will encounter few trawlers. They are large boats (one hundred feet and longer) that fish for shrimp or bottom fish at least fifty miles offshore, dragging a large net deep in the water. Trawlers can most easily be identified by the ramp on the stern where the net is lowered and retrieved, and by large metal rectangles (trawl doors), which will be stowed near the stern while the boat is not fishing. Some trawlers also double as king crab boats (identified by big, boxlike crab pots piled on the stern).

TROLLERS

Trollers are the most common boats along the coast and are the backbone of the individually owned and operated fishing business. These twenty-five to fifty-foot boats are distinguished by two long poles pointing skyward on either

Troller with poles extended for fishing

side of a central mast. The poles are lowered to about a forty-five degree angle to fish. Stainless steel cables run out from power winches (called *gurdies*) and drop from the trolling poles into the water. At the end of each cable is a large weight called a cannonball. Above the cannonball are hooks with lures or bait.

Trollers fish for salmon by motoring along slowly. Depending on the kind of salmon sought, line will be paid out to varying distances from the bottom. For king (Chinook) salmon, a troller will try to skim the cannonballs just over the bottom. He (or often, she) will work from the trolling cockpit, an area of the stern near the gurdies which has remote steering (usually an autopilot), an engine throttle, a fathometer, and an array of extra spreads (lure-and-hook assemblies) and bait.

Fishing near the bottom is trying work, as the troller has to be aware of how much line is out and watch the fathometer closely. If the cannonball hits bottom, the only alternative is to speed up to sweep the lines back. If the gear fouls on the bottom, the cannonball is supposed to break loose to save the rest. But occasionally the rig snags on the bottom, snapping the cable and breaking trolling poles, a loss of hundreds of dollars worth of gear.

When a fish takes one of the hooks, the fisherman will be alerted by bells on the trolling pole. The line is winched in, the fisherman removing each hook-and-lure spread in sequence until the fish is landed.

By using an autopilot, one person can manage the gear alone while the boat steers itself. Most trollers are manned by just one or two people (including many husband-wife teams).

Hand-trollers (identified by the letters "HT" on the cabin's side) look like other trollers except that the boats are smaller and the gurdies are not powered, but cranked by hand. Until 1982, there was no limit on the number of hand-troll permits issued; any Alaska resident with a few dollars could buy one and become a commercial fisherman.

Hand-trolling is especially interesting because it attracts all sorts of people in almost anything that floats: counterculturists supplementing their subsistence life-style with a bit of fishing in rotting hulks, city folks of ample means writing off their sailboats as business ventures via a few weekends of hand-trolling, octogenarian pioneers in well-worn skiffs. The hand-trolling fleet has never been an economically important part of the fishery, but is an important expression of the independence of life-style that Alaskans treasure.

GILL-NETTERS

These boats are almost as common as trollers, and many are outfitted to troll as well as gill net. Gill-netters have a four- or five-foot-diameter drum on which the net is wound and a set of rollers over which the net is paid out or reeled in. Around Puget Sound, most gill-netters are "bow-pickers," who deploy their nets over the bow. On the North Coast, most nets run over the stern. The boats are between twenty-five and thirty-five feet long.

This gill-netter is also licensed for hand-trolling

Gill-netters fish by drifting with the tide, usually close to shore. The extended net floats vertically and is designed to be invisible to salmon. As the fish swim through it, their gills are caught in the fine mesh. Fishermen usually have several nets of varying mesh size, each designed to catch a different species of salmon.

The gill-netter's main hazard is a net snagged on submerged rocks, but too many fish in the web also can sink the net. The number of gill nets found on North Coast beaches attests to the frequency with which these accidents occur.

PURSE SEINERS

These are the biggest of the boats that fish close to shore. In Alaska, seiners cannot be more than sixty feet long. Most are just under that length, and thus called *limit seiners.* Seining is an expensive but lucrative fishing operation. Many purse seiners are owned by fish packing companies and leased to skippers who hire their own crews of about six, with the company getting a share of the profit.

In British Columbia, seiners have a large drum (much larger than a gill-netter's) on the stern. But fish conservation policy does not allow the efficient drum seiners to be used in Alaska. Seiners that fish Southeast waters use a large, hydraulically driven pulley (or power block) on the end of a boom to deploy the net, which is simply piled on the stern deck.

To fish, the seiner sets the net in either a straight line or an open circle. An ungainly looking motorboat called a seine-skiff is used to hold the end of the net in place while the seiner pulls the other end around to close the circle. Then the

Power-block seiners at Craig, Alaska

bottom of the net is drawn inward *(pursed)* to form a bag in which the salmon are trapped. The net then is brought in and lifted aboard.

Jellyfish are the bane of the seiner crew as well as the gill-netter. On power-block seiners, the net comes in high overhead, cascading the gelatinous, stinging creatures onto the crew. This is why you often see them working in complete foul-weather gear and face masks despite the finest weather.

LONG-LINERS

A funnellike chute on the stern, a dozen or more rusty anchors, balloonlike buoys, and a clutch of long poles with flags on them distinguish long-liners. They also are called *halibut boats,* since that is their prey. You will rarely see them working, since they often fish over seamounts many miles offshore. Long lines called *skates* are used, each rigged with many baited hooks. The line is anchored to the bottom and marked with a buoy and pole. The boat sets many of these, returning for them a number of hours later.

TENDERS

Since fishermen often operate far from processing plants, they are served by larger boats called tenders, which rendezvous with fishing boats to pick up their catch and deliver it to a plant. Most tenders are owned by packing companies and buy fish from the fishermen on the spot. Many boats arrange with a packing company and one of its tenders to buy their fish throughout the season. Others sell their catch to whatever packer is handy at the time. Tenders also

Victory, *a packing company tender, unloads at Hoonah, Alaska.*

perform such important services as bringing the fishermen mail, fuel, and groceries.

Fish-Buying Scows

Near important fishing grounds, packing companies will anchor fish-buying scows for the season. These can handle more fish than the tenders and usually have a freezer plant to preserve the fish until a large tender takes them to the processing plant.

In some anchorages, you see two or more scows, each from a different packing company. Competition for fish can get fierce, though prices stay quite constant. For incentives, scows offer free beer or hard liquor, surprisingly diverse and inexpensive groceries, showers, and even saunas.

They are generally willing to sell groceries to kayakers and may let you take a shower at a time when the fishing boats are not in. Many scows are not allowed to sell you fish. Buy, instead, from a fishing boat that is waiting its turn to pitch the day's catch onto the scow's scales.

Limited Entry, Openings, and Closures

Though harvests of salmon and halibut have been fairly good in recent years, there still are too many fishermen chasing too few fish. Consequently, the managing agencies, the Alaska Department of Fish and Game and the B.C.

Fish and Wildlife Branch, Ministry of Environment, have taken various steps to limit the numbers of fishing vessels and their harvest.

In Alaska, the number of fishing permits is limited. The person who wants to fish commercially must buy a permit from someone else. Power-trolling permits currently cost from $15,000 to $25,000 and hand-trolling permits, $1,000 or more. In Southwestern Alaska's Bristol Bay, a gill-net permit can sell for up to $100,000!

Alaska's salmon harvest is regulated by complex schedules of openings and closures of different areas to trolling, gill-netting, and seining. This means long hours of intense work, followed by periods of costly inactivity for boats and crew. Some combination troller—gill-netters will troll in an area until it closes, then pick up their gill net (which cannot be on board while trolling) and race fifty miles or more to catch a gill-net opening somewhere else.

The assorted regulatory controls have substantially increased the costs of fishing and many of the less efficient boats and less savvy fishermen have been driven out of the business. Luck plays a big part in determining whether a season comes out in the black or the red. Fishermen without the wherewithal or gambling spirit to last through a few bad years drop out.

Northwest Coast Indians

The presence of the Indians and their heritage is strongly felt on the North Coast, probably more so than in any other region of North America. Especially in Alaska, where there was no successful military conquest by whites and where no treaties forfeiting Indian rights were signed, the original residents have remained in most of the places where they were living and the people have retained their unique identity and traditional life-styles.

There are six major cultural groupings along the coast between Puget Sound and South Central Alaska.

Coast Salish occupied most of western Washington State and both sides of the Strait of Georgia as far north as Johnstone Strait. Today, diverse tribes include the Makah, Lummi, Duwamish, and many others.

Nootka reside on the west coast of Vancouver Island.

Kwakiutl (pronounced Kwa-*cute*-ill) cover a large area from northern Vancouver Island along the Inside Passage north of Campbell River to Milbanke Sound.

Tsimshian (*Chim*-shin) reside on the northern B.C. coast from Milbanke Sound to Prince Rupert, excluding the Queen Charlottes. In 1887, the Reverend William Duncan received permission to move his religious following of Tsimshians from the Prince Rupert area to Annette Island in Alaska, there establishing the community of Metlakatla. The Tsimshian were not original inhabitants of what is now Southeast Alaska, and the Annette Island community of about twelve hundred is the only U.S. contingent of Tsimshian.

Haida (*Hy*-da) originally lived only in the Queen Charlotte Islands. In the eighteenth century, some of the Haida moved to the southern half of Prince of Wales Island, displacing the Tlingits in the area. About nine hundred Haida now live in that part of Alaska, centered about the community of Hydaburg.

Tlingit (*Clink*-it) inhabit most of Southeast Alaska and parts north, beyond Yakutat.

The Northwest Indians developed a rich and highly effective culture for living on the waterways and outer coast. The marine environment provided a year-round abundance of food and the coastal forests an extraordinary source of working materials. Since the coastal-dwelling Indians were not nomadic, as were the hunting-based cultures of the interior, they developed a material culture of housing, boats, and art that distinguishes them to this day. The western red cedar was the primary material, used in split boards for immense long-houses, canoes up to seventy feet long, and carved totems. The remarkable longevity of cedar accounts for the existence of remnants of their work in long deserted villages to this day.

The coast-dwelling Indians of the north also were great voyagers. The Haida regularly made hundred-odd-mile crossings from the Queen Charlottes to Vancouver Island, and often raided the Puget Sound area for Salish slaves.

Today, almost half of the smaller towns on the North Coast are native communities, among them Skidegate (pronounced *Skid*-i-git), Bella Bella, Klawock, Hydaburg, Angoon, Hoonah, and many others. Non-Indians are in the minority there, and tribal identities run strong. There used to be many more native settlements, but following the ravages of smallpox and other diseases in the late nineteenth century and the region-wide pattern toward consolidated settlements, those gradually were abandoned in favor of jobs and better education and health care in larger communities.

In B.C., most of these small sites are reserves (and so marked on the charts). In Alaska, there had been no lasting settlement of Indian land claims until the 1970s. The culmination was probably the most important act for all Alaskans, native or nonnative—the Alaska Native Claims Settlement Act of 1971 (ANCSA).

Since its purchase from Russia in 1867 until the late nineteenth century, Alaska had existed in a political vacuum, during which its native people were divested of their land rights without benefit of even bogus legality. Soon after the turn of the century, the Tlingits began a long and tenacious campaign to recover their ancestral lands. In 1935, Congress recognized their right to sue for lands taken by the federal government. But for decades after that, nothing happened. When Alaska became a state in 1958, it was given the right to select for state use more than a million acres of federal land. But the selection process soon was brought to a halt by outstanding native claims that rapidly accumulated in the courts as the varied native nations united in pursuit of their land.

They gained an unlikely but powerful ally in the oil companies. Realizing that the North Slope oil discoveries could not be exploited until the native claims were settled, the companies' lobbies made the crucial difference in forcing Congress to act in 1971, granting the largest settlement ever made to aboriginal people in the United States: almost a billion dollars and forty million acres of land.

Both the natives and the state of Alaska have gone ahead with their land selections, which in Southeast have been taken primarily from the Tongass National Forest. The effects of these selections and the changes they will bring to all residents of the region are just beginning to be felt.

Public Land
Management on the North Coast

BRITISH COLUMBIA

Most of the lands along the B.C. coast are Crown lands, deeded to the province by the federal government at the time of Canada's confederation. Management of Crown lands is the responsibility of the B.C. Forest Service within the province's Ministry of Forests. The federal government's land management role on the coast is limited to west Vancouver Island's Pacific Rim National Park.

Logging has been intensive here and there along the coast, primarily on Vancouver Island, the Queen Charlottes, and in the vicinity of Prince Rupert and Kitimat (where there is a large pulp and paper mill). Some of this logging is done on private lands purchased from the province some years ago, but the majority of timber harvesting is done on Crown land leased from the province by such large companies as Crown Zellerbach and MacMillan-Bloedel. Occasionally you will run across small-scale operators (called hand-loggers) taking logs along the shore, as provided by special permits for such harvests.

There is no formal wilderness designation in B.C. Because of remoteness, many of the larger provincial parks remain pristine, although there is no legal mandate to keep them so. The closest equivalent to wilderness management is the province's Ecological Reserve system. A number of preserves scattered along the coast help to perpetuate communities of wildlife or vegetation for scientific study. Although recreation is allowed in some of the reserves, it is not encouraged. For current information on the sites and their uses, write to the Lands Branch, B.C. Ministry of Lands, Parks, and Housing.

The great majority of the B.C. coast is de facto wilderness—wild because there is no pressure to develop it. Along the central coast, north of Queen Charlotte Sound and south of the Prince Rupert–Kitimat area, there is little immediate prospect for change.

But the Prince Rupert area is scheduled for major development in the near future. A major port will be constructed for shipment of wheat from the interior, and a large potash mining development is likely for Ridley Island, a few miles south of Prince Rupert.

Even the remote Queen Charlottes are changing. There is more logging, and recreational use by kayakers, sailors, and charter boats has greatly increased in the late 1970s and early '80s. Growing interest in the abandoned Haida village sites in the Charlottes has prompted the tribe to tighten its control over public access to them. Permits to visit the sites may be obtained from the Skidegate Band of the Haida and from the Parks Division, Ministry of Lands, Parks, and Housing.

ALASKA

The federal government is the great land baron of Southeast Alaska, where the vast majority of the region still is under federal jurisdiction. Well over half of the federal land is in the Tongass National Forest, making the Forest Service the most powerful decision-making agency in the region. All of the local industries and most residents are affected by its policies to at least some extent.

The predominance of federal land makes living in Southeast something of a paradox. Though wild, undeveloped land is everywhere, it has been very difficult to obtain a homesite outside of the major communities. But that is beginning to change. In 1980, the state began to sell some of its land to Alaskan residents, either through a homesite-application procedure (with ownership awarded on the basis of how long the applicants have lived in Alaska) or a lottery (in which you can win the right to buy a parcel at appraised value). As a result, the buds of future suburbia are peeking forth near some communities, such as Petersburg, where new homesites overlook the Wrangell Narrows.

The timber industry is the mainstay of Southeast Alaska's economy (although federal, state, and local governments are the biggest employers). Since almost all of the region's timber is exported, primarily to Japan as pulp and paper, Alaska's forest products economy reflects world markets rather than the U.S. housing market. But in 1982, declining world markets leave Alaska no better off than timber-based regions elsewhere in the country. Though there are small sawmills located throughout the region and a big one in Wrangell, much of the timber goes to two giants for pulp, Ketchikan Pulp Company in Ward Cove and the Japanese-owned Alaska Lumber and Pulp Company in Sitka. The industry depends almost entirely on timber purchased from national forest land. Some of the most intensive logging and extensive haul-road systems are on Prince of Wales Island.

The effects of the 1971 Alaska Native Claims Settlement Act were as significant for the management of federal lands as they were for the natives themselves. Section 17(d)(2) of the act authorized the Department of the Interior to set aside up to eighty million acres of federal land in Alaska that seem suitable for national forests, parks, wildlife refuges, or designation as wild and scenic rivers. These were the so-called "D-2 Lands." Congress was given until the end of 1978 to act on them. Years of hot legislative debate followed, pitting preservationists against opponents of "land lock-ups." The deadline arrived without agreement on legislation. President Carter, in effect, extended it by designating fifty-six million acres as national monuments by executive order. Among these was Admiralty Island National Monument. Finally, in 1980, Congress passed the Alaska National Interest Lands Conservation Act, which doubled the sizes of the National Park and National Wildlife Refuge Systems and tripled the acreage of the National Wilderness Preservation System.

In Southeast, Glacier Bay National Monument was enlarged twenty-one percent and redesignated as Glacier Bay National Park and Preserve. Management of the bay itself was little changed, since the additions were on the outer coast to the northwest toward Yakutat. Hunting is allowed in the Preserve portion. Most of the park and preserve was designated as wilderness.

In the Tongass National Forest, more than five million acres—almost a third of the forest—were designated as wilderness. The fourteen wilderness units there range from four thousand acres to over two million acres. The largest unit, Misty Fjords National Monument, became the largest component of the entire National Wilderness Preservation System.

In a wilderness, management must put preservation of natural processes above all other goals. Logging is prohibited, though mineral and petrochemical exploration and possible subsequent exploitation will be allowed until the end of 1983. Recreational use is permitted as long as preservation objectives are not undermined; hunting, fishing, and trapping continue. Though motorized recreation generally is banned in wilderness, exceptions are made for motorboats or aircraft landings where such uses are traditional.

SOME PLACES
TO GO

Short Kayak Trips
in the Puget Sound Area

Before you embark on an extended trip to the north Pacific coast, a shakedown trip or two is invaluable, especially if you have never camped with your kayak. Try an overnight outing with the gear you will take on an extended trip, experimenting with packing your boat and learning how it performs with a heavy load. Though freshwater trips will get you in shape and sharpen your technique, experience on salt water offers the bonus of practice in dealing with tidal currents and waves.

The Puget Sound area offers a wide range of possibilities for day trips or overnight outings on salt water. True wilderness is not to be found there. Second homes and developments dominate the shoreline. Pleasure boats are everywhere year-round; coves and anchorages fill with them on summer nights. But public agencies have set aside substantial amounts of land on both American and Canadian sides of the Sound, and campsites are plentiful.

Here are a few suggestions for places to visit. Further guidance is available in several boating guides to Puget Sound (included in the Appendix).

Paddling north of Orcas Island, San Juan Islands

Kayaking in the Sound is possible all year. Even in winter, temperatures rarely drop below freezing. There are plenty of windless days, though gales are more frequent than in other seasons. Stay tuned to weather reports and plan your trip to avoid long crossings in the off season.

Harbor Touring

A kayak tour will show you sides of a city harbor that few other people can see. Any coastal city with a busy maritime trade provides lots of interesting things to view. Paddle under piers; some are so huge that you will feel as if you have entered a cavern. On a sunny day, find a spot in the shade near where sunlight strikes the water. You will be able to see a surprising abundance of marine life down there on and around the pilings. Paddle past your local shipyard to see what is going on.

In Seattle, I have enjoyed making annual inspections of Elliott Bay by kayak. I launch at the public dock at the foot of Washington Street and paddle south under the piers. Pausing to inspect the Alaska ferries (at least two of which are present during nonsummer months), I continue on to pass judgment on whatever vessels are off-loading at the Port of Seattle terminals, then turn west for an assessment of construction in progress at Lockheed and Todd Shipyards. Then, weather permitting, I cross Elliott Bay to Pier 56, where I go ashore for a well-earned snack at Ivar's Acres of Clams before continuing north toward Pier 70. I have also conducted informative inspections of the Duwamish Waterway and Pier 90 area.

Almost any coastal city would have as interesting a waterfront as Seattle. In fact, New York City lures me back just to view the underside of its Hudson River piers and to paddle the backwaters of Jamaica Bay, forgotten by all but traffickers in hijacked goods, collectors of marine derelicts, and a few bird watchers.

A few notes of caution about harbor tours. Never, ever, pass between a ship and the piles or wharf to which it is berthed, for obvious reasons. Stay away from propellers, no matter how somnolent a ship appears. Avoid openings on ships' sides which may spew hot water or vile effluvia without warning. If you thump your paddle in greeting on the side of a Soviet freighter, expect to hear expletives about hooliganism accompanied by a bucket of water from above and a visit from the harbor police. Stay out of shipyards, no matter how tempting it may appear behind their drydocks. You could be arrested for trespassing. If you paddle under extensive pier systems, do it at low tide or on the falling tide. (I was almost marooned under one by a flood tide.) Watch out for hot steam pipes and exposed wiring overhead. When you get home, wash your boat. It will need it.

*Carrying kayaks for day trips on the ferry is easy, but much
more arduous if you have camping gear, too.*

Carrying Kayaks on Ferries

The extensive Washington State and British Columbia ferry systems provide unique opportunities for getting around Puget Sound. Both ferry systems allow foot passengers to carry on kayaks at no additional charge. You can ride the ferry and then paddle back to your starting point, or ride one ferry and then paddle to a point where you can catch another for the return trip.

Carrying your kayak and gear aboard the ferry requires a bit of planning and exercise, so arrive early. You will be carrying the kayak onto the car deck, probably stashing it in an out-of-the-way nook on the far end. Since foot passengers usually board via a separate ramp from cars, you will need to touch base with the purser or deckhands before the ferry starts loading to let them know what you have in mind. They will probably want you to carry your boat and duffel aboard just after the departing traffic has left and before the new herd is boarded. Locate yourself and equipment as near as possible to the boarding ramp, wait for their signal, then move quickly to avoid delaying loading the cars.

If you are carrying only the equipment for a day trip, you can probably put some of it in your kayak and carry the rest in a backpack, thus loading in one strenuous trip. If you are camping, you will likely have too much weight to carry in a single trip; it is well over a hundred yards from the boarding ramp to the far end of the big ferries. Ask the deckhands how to make the two trips with the least disruption (or recruit other foot passengers to help carry your gear).

You will probably be asked to get off before the cars do. In the San Juan Islands, the ferries make only brief stops, and off-loading takes some fast footwork. On one trip, a deckhand suggested that my companion and I hitch a ride on an empty flatbed truck that was going ashore at our destination, Shaw Island. The driver agreed, and thus we disembarked with no delay.

Paddling From Winslow to Bremerton via Seattle Ferries
(NOAA Nautical Chart 18445)

Here is an opportunity to take advantage of the extensiveness of the ferry system. Leave your car in downtown Seattle, take the ferry to Winslow on Bainbridge Island, paddle to Bremerton (about nine miles) to catch the ferry back to town. The whole trip can be done in a day, with ferry fares totaling $2.90 per person. (The most expensive part for me was the $6 I spent to park my car downtown for the day!) You could also add a two-mile detour to Blake Island State Park to camp.

Getting to the water at the Winslow ferry landing is a bit of a problem since chainlink fence encloses the terminal grounds. I had to carry my kayak into the parking lot and around a building, then slither down the bank to the beach below the ferry dock. Hug the shore between Winslow (Eagle Harbor) and Restoration Point to avoid ferry traffic. The paddle from Restoration Point to Rich Passage along Bainbridge Island is easy, with plenty of spots to get out for a picnic, particularly at Fort Ward State Park. Since the ebb tide in Rich Passage can flow at over three knots, try to catch the slack or the flood tides. If you must push through against the ebb, the current is much weaker along the shores. Travel as close to either shore as you can without running aground. Even so, expect a workout for the better part of a mile. In Port Orchard, the current is negligible, and you can cross to Bremerton wherever you wish. A float near the ferry dock provides an easy haul-out.

Deception Pass
(NOAA Nautical Chart 18423)

The north end of Whidbey Island offers a variety of extremes for sea kayaking practice—a fast tidal current or easy cruises to island state parks to camp.

WINSLOW AND BREMERTON AREA

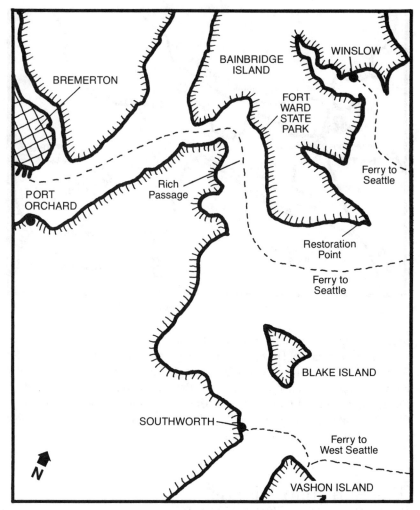

(not for navigation purposes)

Deception Pass is a narrow cut through which the vast waterway behind northern Whidbey Island drains and floods on each tide. Currents may run at up to seven knots, with a complex system of eddies, rips, boils, holes, and even small whirlpools. It is no place for a novice kayaker or someone with a new and unfamiliar boat, but is a good place for an experienced sea kayaker to develop skills for using eddies and riding tidal streams. Beforehand, scout the area from shore, and keep in mind that the currents may increase.(Consult the tide table.)

Five miles east of Deception Pass are Skagit and Hope islands, both undeveloped state parks on which camping is permitted. Both islands have

DECEPTION PASS AREA

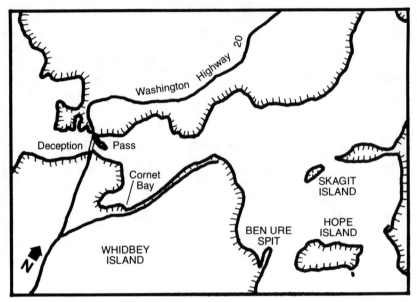

(not for navigation purposes)

primitive campsites with pit toilets. Bring water with you.

The waters east of Deception Pass usually are calmer than in open Puget Sound, though southeast winds from Skagit Bay can be fierce, especially between Hope Island and Ben Ure Spit. Put-ins can be made to the east on Fidalgo Island near La Conner, or at Cornet Bay on Whidbey Island. From Cornet Bay, it is a two- or three-mile paddle to the islands (against a negotiably moderate current if you are running counter to the tide).

The San Juan Islands
(NOAA Nautical Chart 18423)

Washington State ferries make four stops in the San Juan Islands, giving kayakers many options for trips and allowing them to use the ferry either for intermediate hops or to return to Anacortes in the United States or to Sidney on the Canadian side. Eight state parks in the San Juans afford campsites and pleasant stops for picnicking and stretching your legs.

Tidal currents in the islands are strong and complex. You will see sailboats getting nowhere in them or waiting at anchor for slack water. But kayaks can take advantage of the weaker streams or eddies close to the rocky shores. A

Northern Portion of the San Juan Islands

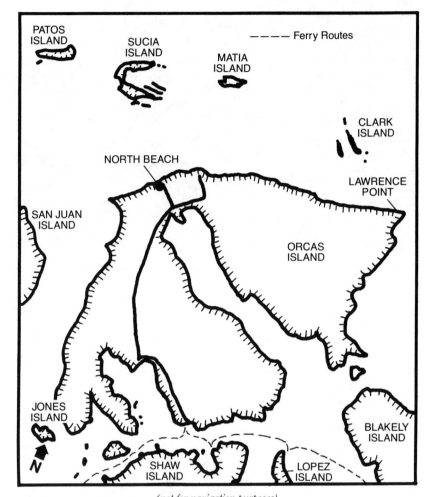

(not for navigation purposes)

current table for the area is valuable, since the currents often shift at different times than does the tide.

Sucia, Matia, and Clark islands are popular kayak destinations. (Also see Werner Furrer's *Water Trails in Western Washington.*) All have state parks, with a developed campground on Sucia, and other, more primitive campsites on all three islands. Water is available on Sucia and Matia, but not on Clark. Lying north of Orcas Island, the islands are reached by a two-mile open crossing. (Consider the weather forecast as you plan this one.) The put-in point on Orcas Island's north shore is several miles' drive from the ferry landing, so you will have to take a car on the ferry to get there (or plan to make a fifteen-mile paddle

Unloading at North Beach after a trip to Sucia Island

from the ferry dock around Orcas's west shore). From the North Beach put-in, a nice loop trip could be made by paddling east along the north shore of Orcas and then crossing near Lawrence Point (watch the rips off the point) to camp on Clark Island. (Bring water with you.) A leisurely trip the next day could bring you to a second camp on either Matia or Sucia, with a crossing back to North Beach the third day.

JONES ISLAND STATE PARK

Jones Island State Park, just west of Orcas Island, is well suited for a kayak trip. The four-mile paddle from either the Orcas or Shaw Island landing is in protected water, with only the last half-mile, the crossing of Spring Passage to Jones Island, exposed to southerly winds. In good weather, kayakers could continue to Friday Harbor to catch the return ferry. If you had left a car at Orcas Island, a circle route to Jones and then south around Shaw Island via Friday Harbor would be a pleasant sixteen-mile overnight trip, with the option of camping a second night at Turn Island State Park west of Friday Harbor. (No water is available at Turn.)

SOUTH LOPEZ ISLAND

Want a taste of the outside coast? The south end of Lopez Island reminds me more of the outer coast than anywhere else in Puget Sound. The coastline around Iceberg Point is rocky and convoluted, with many offshore rocks and

SOUTHERN PORTION OF THE SAN JUAN ISLANDS

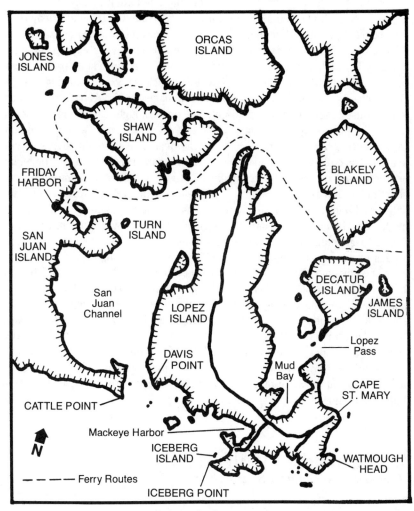

(not for navigation purposes)

islets, tiny coves choked with jackstrawed logs, and big kelp beds. A strong westerly wind flowing through the Strait of Juan de Fuca can produce swells at Iceberg Point that rival the open Pacific. But this dose of heavy water comes in moderation: a mile north or south of the point and you are back in the placid waters more characteristic of the San Juans.

An easy day trip can be made to Iceberg Point from Mackeye Harbor. Better yet, make a longish fourteen-mile day trip from Mackeye Harbor around the point, east to Watmough Head, then north to Lopez Pass, and ending in Mud Bay, with a three-quarter-mile hike back to retrieve your car. The coast between Iceberg Point and Cape St. Mary is worth it.

A thirty-mile multiday trip could be made between Friday Harbor and Lopez ferry dock via Iceberg Point. Carry kayaks onto the ferry to Friday Harbor and paddle south in San Juan Channel. Camping on southern Lopez Island is a bit of a problem because there is little public land. An early camp could be made at Turn Island just south of Friday Harbor. There is a state park on Iceberg Island, but this barren hundred-yard-long rock is poor for camping and has no good haul-out. The U.S. Bureau of Land Management holds Iceberg Point as a lighthouse reservation, but haul-outs are poor though feasible on the north side of the point in good weather. The other alternative is to seek permission from waterfront landowners to camp on the beach, guaranteeing that you will leave no trace of your stay. Some will accommodate a small group of congenial boaters; many others will not. Finally, a detour could be made along the west shore of Decatur Island to camp at James Island State Park (no water available), and then head west through Thatcher Pass to the Lopez ferry landing. You might consider crossing Rosario Strait to Fidalgo Head if you left your car at the Anacortes terminal, but only in very calm weather and just before the slack tide so that the strong currents off Fidalgo Head can be minimized.

The currents run very strong at the southern mouth of San Juan Channel between Cattle and Davis Points, so plan to pass through on the slack or a favorable tide. If you must, an opposing current can be bested by hugging the east shore. It is a good place to practice working the eddies. Be careful, as the rips behind Deadman Island are particularly boisterous. Within a few feet of the rocks on the Lopez shore are slower currents, still eddies in which to rest, and even some reverse current eddies, though the main stream races by just inches away. Keep your bow out of it, or you will be whipped around and downstream before you know it.

The Canadian Gulf Islands
(Canadian Hydrographic Service Chart 3310)

On the Canadian side of the southern Strait of Georgia are the Gulf Islands, equal in beauty to the San Juans. The rain shadow effect from Vancouver Island minimizes rainfall in the countless islands forested with fir and madrona, and there is little underbrush to impede strolling about. As in the San Juans, currents are fast and require paddling in tune with the tide cycles.

Ferry systems (assorted local runs in addition to the B.C. ferries) are extensive and will allow foot passengers to carry kayaks, thereby making loops interconnected by ferry rides an intriguing possibility. From the U.S. side, trips to the Gulf Islands are restricted by the need to clear Canadian Customs at Sidney or at Bedwell Harbour on South Pender Island. (The latter is only open

Southern Portion of the Canadian Gulf Islands

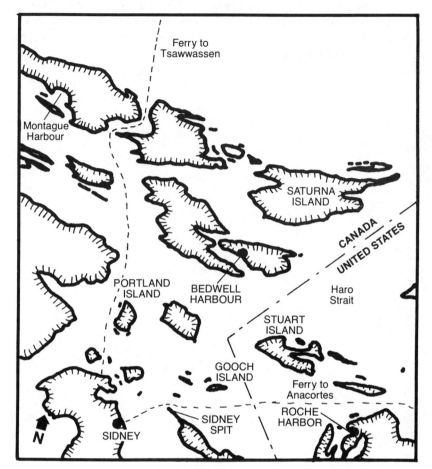

(not for navigation purposes)

from the middle of May until the middle of September.) If you cross Haro Strait at the narrowest points (i.e., Patos Island to Saturna Island or Stuart Island to Gooch Island), do not get out of your boat until you reach the customs station. Otherwise, Canadian officials may confiscate your boat and subject you to charges. The same applies in crossing from Canada to the U.S. in the San Juans; you must first land at either Roche Harbor or Friday Harbor and report to customs.

There is an extensive Marine Provincial Park system in the Gulf Islands. Some parks, such as Montague Harbour and Sidney Spit Marine Parks, have developed campgrounds. The majority are undeveloped. You can camp, but there is no water and you may not build fires. (Bring a stove.)

Portland Island is one undeveloped park which makes an excellent trip destination from Sidney. (Foot passengers from the mainland could carry kayaks over on the ferries from Anacortes in the U.S. or Tsawwassen in B.C. and launch them at Sidney.) The island lies about four miles from Sidney. There is a nice beach for landing on the south side. Underbrush on the island is kept down by grazing sheep. Bring water and a cooking stove.

Wrangell to Petersburg
via Wrangell Narrows

OVERVIEW: This is an easy three- to five-day trip of about forty miles in protected waters along a major marine traffic route. Wrangell Narrows is famous for its twisting channel, where the strong current races and the tight clearances between rocks have claimed many a ship. None of the currents is particularly dangerous for kayakers. Marine traffic, which has very little room in which to maneuver, is the only hazard. Kayaks can easily keep to the safety of the shallows along the sides. Because of the heavy marine traffic, logging, and shore developments, brown bears are rare along this route.

ACCESS: Alaska ferries or Alaska Airlines to Wrangell and from Petersburg.

SUPPLY POINTS: Wrangell and Petersburg.

CHARTS AND OTHER NAVIGATION AIDS: NOAA charts 17375 (detail of Wrangell Narrows), 17382; current tables for Wrangell Narrows and local points.

Kayak and barges in Wrangell Narrows

WRANGELL NARROWS

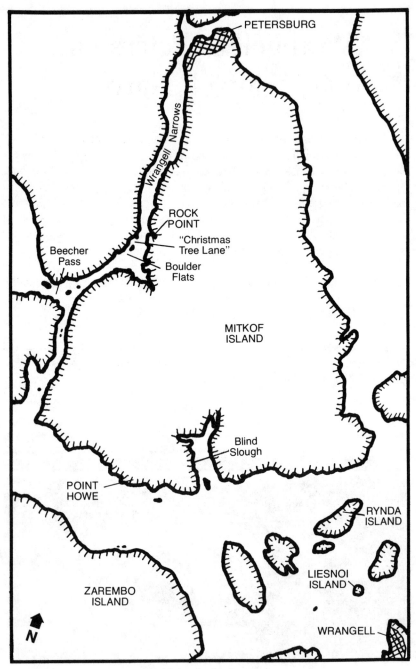

(not for navigation purposes)

From Wrangell, head northwest to Liesnoi and Rynda Islands. (Paddling by way of Zarembo Island in calm weather is an alternate route.) Currents north and west of Wrangell are strong (setting southwest on the ebb and northeast on the flood), so start on the slack to avoid extra work.

On Mitkof Island, a road from Petersburg follows the shore east of Blind Slough. Traffic is frequent on weekends, with motor homes and campers gathering at one beachside campsite a few miles east of the slough. The coast of the island to the west of the slough is largely unroaded and wild, except for a few clearcuts and a logging camp near Point Howe.

Wrangell Narrows must be navigated in concert with the tide, although the current is slow enough to paddle against for the first few miles at the southern entrance.

Understanding the current schedules in the Narrows takes careful study of the tables. Use Wrangell Narrows reference station tables, but note that these are based on the north end at Petersburg. Then see the tables for secondary stations in Wrangell Narrows to determine the current changes at the southern end.

At both ends of the Narrows, the currents flow inward (toward each other) on the flood tides and away from each other on the ebbs, filling or draining from both ends. Changes at the southern end and center generally are about twenty minutes behind Petersburg (though I found them delayed as much as an hour when I passed through). The currents average about two knots from the southern end to Beecher Pass, and may run as fast as seven knots between Beecher Pass and Boulder Flats. The currents meet just north of Rock Point, about midway through the Narrows. It is possible to enter the south end just before the flood current, ride it to the middle, and then catch the ebb north to Petersburg, though you will have to keep moving and paddle steadily on the northern third. Currents are negligible through most of that third, increasing just before Petersburg.

The area between Beecher Pass and Rock Point presents a real challenge to large vessels. The Alaska ferry *Columbia* is the largest ship that can use the Narrows; cruise ships have to take another route. The *Columbia* can go through only at midtide or higher, and then the water will be only five feet deep under her keel. Since the ship "squats" lower at the stern when underway, she has to go through slowly. At one point, aptly named Threading the Needle, the 85-foot-wide ferry must negotiate a channel only 120 feet wide. The crew are specially licensed for the Narrows, and two lookouts are posted on the bow. If you meet any large vessels, stand aside; they cannot go around you.

In the Narrows' twenty-one miles, there are more than seventy navigation aids, fifty-four of which are lighted. The area north of Boulder Flats is called "Christmas Tree Lane," and that is what it looks like at night, with lights marking the eastern edge of the channel.

Camping is best toward the southern end of the Narrows. Homes dot the shorelines of the northern half. Much of the area north of Beecher Pass recently was sold for homesites through the state's land lottery. Camp with respect for that private property, and leave no trace of your stay.

Campsites are not easy to find near Petersburg. (There is a campground not far from the airport but it is not on the water.) There are nice showers and a sauna available for a fee at the Nordic Travel Agency in town.

Hoonah to Tenakee
via Tenakee Portage

OVERVIEW: This forty-mile route takes you over a short portage that con-
nects Tenakee Inlet with Port Frederick, an arm of Icy Strait. The portage is an
ancient one, originally used by local Tlingits and later by the Russians. John
Muir, the naturalist and founder of the Sierra Club, camped at the portage in
1879 on his way north to Glacier Bay. Later, local fishermen improved the por-
tage-way, across which they carried their fishing boats.

The journey begins at Hoonah, a Tlingit village just off Icy Strait, and ends

*On the northern side, the last quarter-mile approach to the portage
is along this creeklike slough that floods only on the high tide.*

HOONAH TO TENAKEE VIA TENAKEE PORTAGE

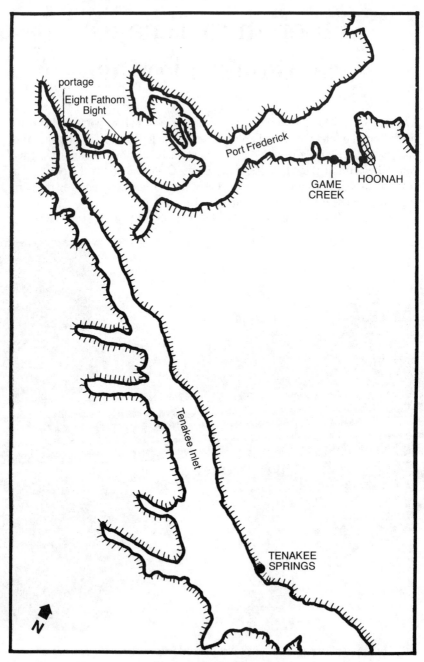

(not for navigation purposes)

in the picturesque community of Tenakee Springs. There are no cars in Tenakee, which cannot be reached by road. That contributes to the leisurely pace of community life, which centers around the public bathhouse over the hot springs. Though you will see signs of logging here and there along the way, buildings and other boats are rare. Brown bears are common all along the route, especially in the river estuaries on the southern shore of Tenakee Inlet.

ACCESS: Alaska ferry to Hoonah and from Tenakee Springs. Ferries run less frequently to Tenakee than to Hoonah, so plan around the pick-up connection as well as around the tides.

SUPPLY POINTS: Hoonah and Tenakee.

CHARTS AND OTHER NAVIGATION AIDS: NOAA charts 17302 (for detail of Port Frederick and the portage) and 17300 (a very small-scale chart of the entire area). There is no large-scale chart for Tenakee Inlet. A tide table is essential for catching high water at the portage.

From Hoonah, follow either shore south into Port Frederick. On the west shore at Game Creek, you will pass the agricultural community of Mount Bether Bible Center, one of the few places along the North Coast where grazing cattle and horses are seen. This religious community has been quite successful, selling its surplus produce in local markets around the region.

As you paddle deeper into Port Frederick, there are fine views of the peaks of Chichagof Island both in front and beyond Tenakee Inlet. It seems hard to believe that you will find a waterway through the rugged country ahead. Though it retains much of its beauty, the western part of Port Frederick is being logged, and there is a large logging camp on the north shore at Eight Fathom Bight.

Some current may be encountered in the last mile or two before the portage. Try to arrive at the final portion on the rising tide, not only to ride with the current, but also to use the water at its highest point to get as far as possible.

The last mile approaching the portage is very shallow, and a spring tide is needed to get all the way. Apparently, the portage was easier to negotiate in past years than it is now. Louis L'Amour's novel, *Sitka,* includes an episode in which a schooner is dragged across. Viewing the portage, that seems unlikely. But Chart 17302 bears a notation that "shoaling amounting to as much as six feet occurred locally due to the 1958 Alaska earthquake." It is possible that the land around the portage rose that much, and vegetation patterns on both sides of the portage suggest that to be the case.

The approach culminates in a slough that floods only on spring tides. If you cannot arrange to be there for one, you will just have to carry your kayak a hundred yards or so across a grassy area to the last pond in the slough (and much farther if you miss high tide). Beware the black, oozy "quick mud" along the pond's shore at the portage.

Many people miss the turn into the slough. Indeed, it does not look like anything more than the mouth of a creek. But stay to the right and follow the tiny channel through the grasses as far as the tide will take you. After extracting yourself from the ooze on the slough's far shore, follow the excavated cut over the low ridge to the shore of Tenakee Inlet just beyond.

Either shore of Tenakee Inlet can be followed east to Tenakee Springs. The south shore, with its numerous bays and stream estuaries, is more scenic, but also longer if you follow the shoreline. Brown bears are more numerous on the south shore than the north. Since much of the land near Tenakee has been purchased through the land lottery, campsites within a few miles of town are becoming increasingly scarce. The town is delightful. Allow a half-day to explore.

At Tenakee Springs the ferry has no auto ramp. At high tide, foot passengers enter and leave the ferry by way of a gangway linking dock and auto deck. Kayaks then present no particular problems. Not so at low tide, when the gangway runs from the dock to the ship's upper deck. A rigid kayak riding on the auto deck must be carried up an interior staircase (no mean feat, and impossible with some boats) or lowered over the ferry's side.

Mud on the portage's north end

Sitka to
Kalinin Bay and Back

OVERVIEW: On this forty-five-mile loop trip beginning on the protected waters of Sitka Sound, you will ride tidal currents through narrow straits to a scenic bay on the fringe of the open Pacific. The return is via a passage negotiable only at high tide and includes a stop at a Forest Service recreation cabin (which can be used by advance reservation). There also is an optional day trip on the open Pacific to a spectacular, beach-fronted cove.

Most of this route is in major marine traffic channels and waters that fishing boats frequent, so the paddler is seldom far from help, if needed. The protected waters without long crossings make this an excellent route for less experienced paddlers. Be alert for brown bears all along the way, especially at the back of Kalinin Bay when salmon are spawning.

ACCESS: Alaska ferry or Alaska Airlines to and from Sitka.

SUPPLY POINTS: Sitka, Kalinin Bay (fish-buying scow with a good stock of groceries, summer only).

CHARTS AND OTHER NAVIGATION AIDS: NOAA charts 17323, 17324, and 17325 (optional), current tables for Surgius Narrows with local point corrections for Neva and Olga Straits.

If you arrive by airline, take a taxi to nearby Mount Edgecumbe High School. The public launching ramps there are ideal for assembling and launching folding boats. It is a short paddle from there across the channel to the public floats, where you can moor while shopping or sight-seeing in Sitka.

There are no stores near the ferry dock at Old Sitka in Starrigavan Bay, six miles to the north. (Buses and taxis shuttle between the terminal and the town whenever a ferry arrives or leaves.) Kayaks can be launched on tide flats near the ferry dock.

From Sitka, paddle north along Lisianski Peninsula toward Olga Strait. Both Olga Strait and the consecutive Neva Strait must be paddled with the current in your favor. Neither current is especially strong or turbulent, but they are fast enough that you will not want to paddle upstream through them. Look up Surgius Narrows in the current tables and make the local corrections for Olga

Sitka Sound to Kalinin Bay

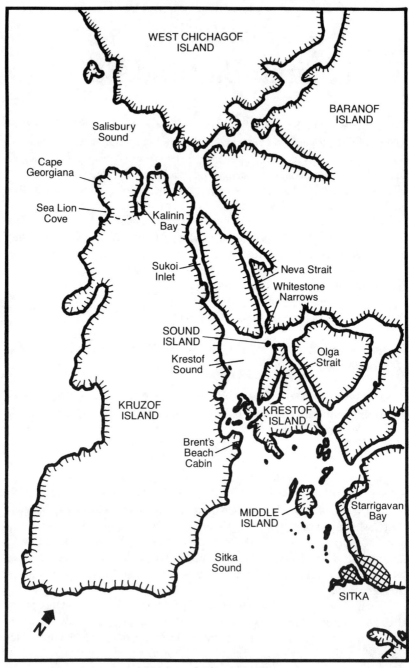

(not for navigation purposes)

and Neva straits.

The two straits flow in opposing directions, with the currents meeting or separating in the middle a half-mile south of Whitestone Narrows. If you enter Olga Strait at the middle of the flood tide, you will arrive at Whitestone Narrows at the tide change. Then you can catch the ebb current through Neva Strait. If you have to wait for the ebb current to start running, you can explore the old World War II coastal artillery installation on Sound Island, which guarded the northern approach to Sitka Sound. Land on the little gravel beach on the northeast corner of the island and follow the overgrown road upward a hundred yards to the blockhouse, which is almost completely hidden by brush.

The deepwater channel in Whitestone Narrows is indeed narrow, so give large vessels a wide berth by staying to the west side.

You will start to feel the Pacific's swells soon after leaving Neva Strait, with the open water of Salisbury Sound ahead. Hug the shore of Kruzof Island as you head west toward Kalinin Bay. There are plenty of coves in which to haul out if the weather should take a turn for the worse.

Kalinin Bay is a jewel, with peaks rising all around, a huge tidal flat where brown bears feed on spawning salmon at the back of the bay, and ruins of an old cannery to explore. Salmon trollers use the bay as an anchorage. The scow anchored at the head of the bay buys their catch and offers showers and groceries.

There are plenty of campsites from which to choose. Most have been "improved" by fishermen and hunters over the years. To minimize both impact on the environment and the chance of meeting up with bears, use the established sites just east of the scow.

Weather permitting, a pleasant day trip can be made around Cape Georgiana to Sea Lion Cove, an exceptionally beautiful bay with a mile-long sandy beach. The round-trip distance is about ten miles. If you do not want to risk paddling on the open Pacific, there is a well-used trail that runs to the cove from the back of Kalinin Bay. A red marker on a tree marks the trailhead. The round-trip hike is about four miles long, with little change in elevation. Be especially cautious about brown bears along the trail.

The sea route to Sea Lion Cove is wide open, with no easy haul-outs between the cove and Point Kruzof. But with a good eye cocked for the weather, this can be an exhilarating test of your open-ocean paddling skills. Waves reflecting off the rocky shore between Kruzof Point and Cape Georgiana produce choppy water near shore; it is much easier paddling farther out. Watch for intermittent breakers over submerged offshore rocks in the area.

There is heavy surf all along the beach in Sea Lion Cove, but a landing can be made through the mouth of the stream at the southern end, where a point jutting seaward provides some protection from the swells in calm or moderate weather.

The return to Sitka from Kalinin Bay can be made by the original route or a more westerly one via Sukoi Inlet. The narrow passage between the inlet and

Sea Lion Cove

Krestof Sound dries at low tide, but is easy going for kayaks at high tide. Since the ebb and flow of water to the ocean are more confined by the narrowness of Sukoi Inlet than by Krestof Sound to the south, expect to fight some current as you paddle through the passage on the flood tide, and to get a lift from the current there on the ebb.

In Krestof Sound, continue south along the shore of either Kruzof or Krestof Island toward the intricate waterways through the Magoun Islands and sandy beaches west and south of Hayward Strait on Kruzof Island. Brent's Beach Cabin, located about three-quarters of a mile south of Hayward Strait, can be reserved for use through the Forest Service's Sitka Area Office.

The route you choose to return to Sitka will depend on weather and your willingness to make an exposed crossing of Sitka Sound. The safest route is a roundabout one to the northeast along Krestof Island to the southern end of Olga Strait, south to Starrigavan Bay, and then following the shoreline to Sitka. In good weather, a crossing can be made eastward from Brent's Beach to the Middle Island group (consult the current table, as moderate currents can make more work for you as you near the islands), and thence southeast through the chain of offshore islands to Sitka. These islands epitomize the beauty of Sitka Sound, bearing the brunt of the Pacific's swells on their westerly shores with more quiet water behind them. There are many short crossings among the islands, where waters can be rough in a southerly or westerly wind. Many of the islands are privately owned. Campsites are few, available only on some of the smallest islands. Bring water with you.

Camping near Sitka is limited to the Forest Service campgrounds at Starrigavan Bay near the ferry landing and at Sawmill Creek, a few miles southeast of town. Neither campground is on the water. Showers can be had at moderate cost in the Sitka Hotel.

Glacier Bay
National Park and Preserve

OVERVIEW: This undisputed mecca for saltwater paddling attracts kayakers from all over the nation, even the world. Easy access for folding boats doubtlessly contributes to its appeal; nowhere else can owners of collapsible boats voyage in such incomparable wilderness yet with so little travel time required to reach the scene. The largely protected waters make it a good place for less experienced paddlers to sharpen their skills.

ACCESS: Alaska ferry to Hoonah (twenty-five miles southeast of Glacier

Folbots drifting in Muir Inlet, Glacier Bay

GLACIER BAY

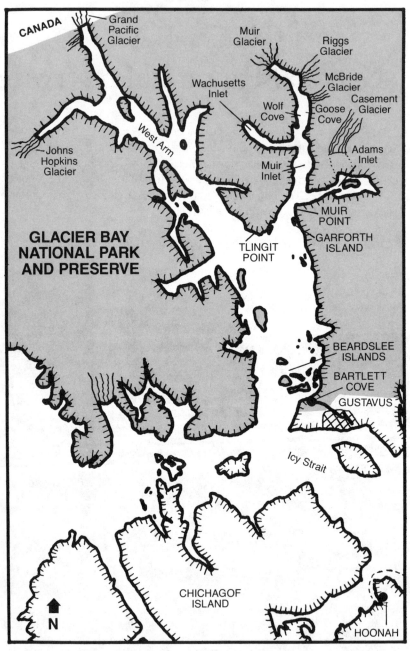

CANADA

Grand Pacific Glacier

Muir Glacier

Riggs Glacier

McBride Glacier

Wachusetts Inlet

Casement Glacier

Wolf Cove

Goose Cove

West Arm

Johns Hopkins Glacier

Adams Inlet

Muir Inlet

GLACIER BAY NATIONAL PARK AND PRESERVE

MUIR POINT

GARFORTH ISLAND

TLINGIT POINT

BEARDSLEE ISLANDS

BARTLETT COVE

GUSTAVUS

Icy Strait

N

CHICHAGOF ISLAND

HOONAH

(not for navigation purposes)

Bay), Alaska Airlines jet to Gustavus with bus connection to Bartlett Cove, or Channel Flying charter to Bartlett Cove from Juneau.

SUPPLY POINTS: Gustavus or Hoonah; none in Glacier Bay.

CHARTS AND OTHER NAVIGATION AIDS: NOAA chart 17318, current tables for North Inian Pass with local point corrections.

Tidewater glaciers are, of course, the keystone of the Glacier Bay experience, although it encompasses much more. When Captain Vancouver passed through Icy Strait at the end of the eighteenth century, there was no Glacier Bay; ice covered the site. Less than a century later, John Muir found the terminus of the glacier (that now bears his name) had retreated more than twenty miles to the north. Its present location is over forty miles from Icy Strait. During this rapid retreat, remnants of a previous age were uncovered—stumps and logs that had been buried by the last ice advance four thousand years ago. The varying stages of reestablishment of vegetation and animal habitats in the glaciers' wake make a fascinating study area for naturalists. In addition, humpback and killer whales frequently are seen in the bay. There are old-growth forests, undisturbed for centuries, and outer coast bays and inlets that rarely are visited.

Paddlers can find a range of conditions to suit them within the Glacier Bay National Park and Preserve boundaries. Within the bay, waters tend to be quieter than elsewhere in the region, though strong southeast winds in stormy weather and stiff northeasters or westerlies in fair weather can churn up waves of dangerous proportions. Since long crossings are rarely required and places to haul out and camp are plentiful, kayaking in the bay is relatively safe for prudent kayakers. Hazards include ice falling from a glacier's terminus, causing waves that can easily swamp a nearby kayak. Floating icebergs can roll over without notice as melting changes their center of gravity. Because of all the ice, the waters of the bay are colder than elsewhere in Southeast Alaska and the hypothermia threat more severe. Bears, both black and brown, have caused problems for campers in the past, so "bear etiquette" must be observed rigorously when ashore.

Defensive firearms are allowed, as is the case in other national parks in Alaska. Park personnel will seal your weapon in Bartlett Cove so that they can tell if it is fired in the park. Go to the ranger station to have that done.

Fine treatments of Glacier Bay's natural history are found in several books on the area, some of which are listed in the Appendix. Excellent guidance for voyaging into the park's farther reaches appears in Margaret Piggott's *Discover Southeast Alaska with Pack and Paddle,* also referenced in the Appendix. Rather than duplicate these resources, this chapter explains and updates some of the problems of getting to and within Glacier Bay and outlines some travel possibilities along the more popular Muir Inlet routes, leaving exploration in other directions to you.

Getting to Glacier Bay

Glacier Bay is primarily the domain of the folding kayak because there is no surface carrier serving it (partly because the residents of nearby Gustavus wish to avoid the changes that would bring). For rigid kayaks there are two alternatives. The first is to take the Alaska ferry from Juneau to Hoonah (which costs $12 per person). From there, it is a thirty-mile paddle to Bartlett Cove, including at least a three-mile crossing of Icy Strait and about six miles of paddling along the eastern shore of the mouth of Glacier Bay to Bartlett Cove, the park headquarters. Bonnie Kaden of Alaska Discovery in Gustavus feels the crossing of Icy Strait is an extremely dangerous one because of the strong winds that often funnel through the strait, especially if they are contrary to the tidal current. According to Ms. Kaden, few paddlers were able to make the crossing during the summer of 1982 (although I know a few who did). If you decide to do it, be sure to leave plenty of time for getting to Glacier Bay and back and wait for good weather before making an early morning crossing.

The second alternative is to charter Channel Flying's Twin Beech aircraft in Juneau, which has the capacity to carry two rigid kayaks and their paddlers. Call or write for the cost and to make reservations.

For folding boats, air transportation to Glacier Bay is easy. Alaska Airlines has a daily flight to Gustavus, located on the mouth of the bay and outside the national park. Most of the passengers on the flight are tourists coming from all over the world. They will be overnighting at the hotel in Bartlett Cove before taking the tour boat to the head of the bay and departing from Gustavus on the afternoon jet. The minority are hikers or kayakers.

At Gustavus, a bus meets the flight to take passengers the twelve miles to Bartlett Cove, where there are a campground, hotel, and restaurant.

Kayak Rentals in Glacier Bay

Alaska Discovery, based in Gustavus and Juneau, rents K-2 (two-seat) fiberglass kayaks in Bartlett Cove. These Belugas, made by Easy Rider, cost $30 a day. There is a reservation system, and they usually are booked up during the summer. The boats come complete with paddles, spray covers, life jackets, and flotation bags. You must bring the waterproof storage bags for your gear.

People frequently bring frame packs and discover that those will not fit in the kayaks.

Alaska Discovery and the Park Service naturalists give an orientation session for kayak renters in Bartlett Cove, and other kayakers are welcome to attend.

Going Up the Bay

The only glaciers in sight from Bartlett Cove are in the distant and occasionally visible Fairweather Range. Not a few backpackers arrive to find (to their disappointment) that the nearest glaciers still are at least thirty miles away. Some, reluctant to spend nearly a hundred dollars for tour boat transportation to and from the head of the bay, stay a few days at Bartlett Cove and then leave, unglaciated. Hiking in the Bartlett Cove area is quite limited.

Kayakers can, of course, load up and head north to glacier country on their own. If time is limited or if you are not inclined to paddle thirty miles to the glaciers at the head of the bay, the tour boat *Thunder Bay* will take you there and drop you off. You can arrange to be picked up later for the return trip. The round-trip fare (1982) is $79; drop-offs and pickups cost $8 per kayak. Advance reservations are recommended and may be made through Alaska Exploration Holidays in Seattle.

The *Thunder Bay* operates on a very tight schedule, since it must return to Bartlett Cove each day in time for passengers to catch the afternoon jet at Gustavus. Consequently, the boat consolidates pickups and drop-offs at five places: Wolf Cove, McBride Glacier, Riggs Glacier, Muir Point, and (for those going into the West Arm) Tlingit Point. (The number and location of these points may change from year to year.) The *Thunder Bay* has a shallow-draft bow and can nose in to many beaches, discharging hikers or kayakers over a ladder.

Bartlett Cove to Muir Inlet

Before leaving Bartlett Cove, be sure to check in with park personnel at the ranger station a quarter-mile north of the lodge. They can advise you on places to see, current regulations on camping, and such local problems as camp-raiding bears (which sometimes require that problem areas be closed to campers).

The east shore north of Bartlett Cove offers the best protection and fewest crossings and thus is preferred by most paddlers heading up the bay. Just north of the cove are the labyrinthine Beardslee Islands. Since the islands are slowly rising (at a rate of over a foot a decade) due to the glacier's retreat to the north, many of the passages between them are very shallow and dry at low tide. Plan to pass through them at high tide. Drinking water is hard to find in the islands.

North of the Beardslees is a succession of bays and coves interspersed with steep cliffs and precipitous peaks. Mount Wright, just before Adams Inlet, is the home of a large community of mountain goats, which easily can be seen from the water on the western slopes. Garforth Island, just west of Mount Wright, is a popular campsite for kayakers. Though the island is usually bear-free, a maverick black bear caused trouble there in the summer of 1982, brazenly raiding campers' tents.

Adams Inlet provides an exciting and scenic side trip, with a fast ride on the tidal race through the narrows into the pool of the inner inlet. The run is comparable to a fairly easy white-water river, with one rock in the center to be avoided. Consult the tide table for timing and avoid the extrafast currents on big tides.

North of Adams Inlet, the evidence of glaciers becomes increasingly apparent. The country takes on a desolate character, since plant life is in the pioneer stages of reestablishment on the land more recently uncovered by ice. Icebergs float south in a constant procession, with all but the biggest melting by the time they pass Garforth Island. The farther north you go, the thicker they become. Beyond Wachusetts Inlet, the water can become so congested that paddling becomes a matter of finding a course through them. From here north, be careful to avoid being trapped by ice and stay away from larger bergs that may roll over.

You may wish to check in with the backcountry ranger stationed in Goose Cove. Campsites are available in a number of places in the upper inlet. On foot in the upper inlet, watch out for falling glacial ice and rockslides on the surrounding hills. Camp well above the high-tide line and carry your boats well away from the water, as falling ice can cause large waves that sweep above the normal levels. Activities ashore in this area are well described in Margaret Piggott's book.

North Prince of Wales Island, Craig to Petersburg

OVERVIEW: This is a long trip, 130 miles, through island-studded sounds and intricate passages along the west and north coasts of Prince of Wales Island. The journey can be shortened to about eighty miles by concluding at Point Baker.

It will take you to out-of-the-way country, far from major marine traffic routes. Other than the fishing boats that operate near the islands bordering Sumner Strait, you will see few boats along the way. Between logging scars, the country is wild, sparsely populated. It was not always so. Ruins of old mines, canneries, and abandoned communities are common, making this a good place to glimpse the Alaska that used to be early in the century, and also to see the fishing and logging that form the backbone of the region's present-day economy.

On the beach in Sumner Strait east of Point Baker;
Kupreanof Island in the distance

North Prince of Wales Island Area

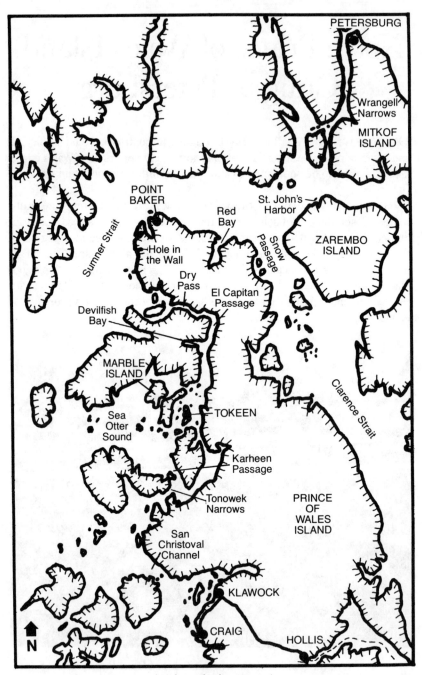

(not for navigation purposes)

ACCESS: Alaska ferry from Ketchikan to Hollis, with connecting bus service (or private transportation) to Craig. At Petersburg, there are daily connections to other points by Alaska ferry or Alaska Airlines.

For those wishing to end the trip at Point Baker, Southeast Alaska Skyways offers a weekly flight from that community to Ketchikan. Since a De Havilland Beaver is used, folding kayaks and excess baggage may require special arrangements and prove expensive. A chartered flight to Petersburg or Wrangell may be more cost effective and convenient.

SUPPLY POINTS: Craig, Klawock, Tokeen (limited), Point Baker.

CHARTS AND OTHER NAVIGATION AIDS: NOAA charts 17403, 17404, 17405, 17387, 17378 (optional), 17381 (optional), 17382, 17375. These omit portions of the coastline between Sumner Strait and Snow Passage. This and all of the above-mentioned charts except 17404 and 17405 are covered by the small-scale chart 17360, which offers a good overview, but little detail because of the large area covered. Current tables will be needed to coordinate with the flows at San Christoval Channel, Tonowek Narrows, Karheen Passage, and Dry Pass.

From Ketchikan, take the Alaska ferry to Hollis. The ferry makes the run three or four times a week. A bus meets the ferry to carry foot passengers the thirty-one miles to Craig. That is the way to get there if you have a folding boat. With a rigid kayak, you will have to make your own arrangements. Write or telephone the Craig City Hall to inquire about transportation possibilities. As an alternative, you can chance hitching a ride with a fellow passenger with a vehicle on the ferry, or, as a final resort, stash your kayak out of sight and above the high-tide line at Hollis, take the bus to Craig, contract with a driver there, and return to Hollis for your boat.

During the summer, Craig is a fisherman's mecca. Seiners, trollers, and others crowd the floats, in from the popular fishing areas around Noyes Island and Dall Island. Stores, repair facilities, and taverns do a thriving business, especially during long fishing closures when the boats may remain in town for as many as four days at a time. (There usually are itinerants wandering the waterfront in search of fishing jobs. Thefts have occurred. Secure your gear while in town.)

From Craig, your course curves northwest through the islands and reefs of San Alberto Bay to San Christoval Channel, which should be negotiated on the ebb tide due to the strong current. Beyond are pleasant, protected channels behind intermittent islands, with humpback whales frequently seen in Tonowek Bay. Both Tonowek Narrows and Karheen Passage have currents too strong to paddle against, so consult your current tables.

A mile or so north of the narrows at Karheen Passage is the site of the abandoned Tlingit village of Karheen. It is in a small cove on Tuxekan Island.

*Seiner crews at work on their nets in Craig during a
period closed to fishing. At left is a seine skiff, used to hold
one end of the net while the parent boat tows the other
end to form a circle.*

Though old logging still scars the area, this is a pleasant place to go ashore to explore. In a small bight just to the south are the remains of an old cannery, which is identified by assorted pieces of rusty machinery that litter the beach. In the dense forest behind are the boiler and other equipment which remained after the cannery buildings burned.

Sea Otter Sound, an island-studded jewel, has a history as active as the present logging that surrounds it. Canneries and salteries once occupied many of the coves. Northwestern Prince of Wales Island is rich in marble, which was shipped from four quarries in the area for buildings as far distant as Utah. The quarry on Marble Island shipped huge blocks to Tacoma, Washington, as late as 1932. (The quarries reportedly make good swimming pools for kayakers who happen by.)

Just north of Sea Otter Sound on El Capitan Island is Tokeen. This was once the largest fish-freezer plant on the West Coast, but the extensive buildings have fallen into dilapidation since the plant was closed in the 1940s. A family bought the property and now makes it their home, with hopes of someday establishing a resort. Theirs is an example of remote life "in the bush." The children went to school by correspondence, and the family earns money to supplement the produce of gardens and sea by selective, small-scale logging and mink-trapping. Since this is now private property, do not feel free to wander around without the owner's permission. A small store in the old freezer plant

Tokeen

carries a limited stock of supplies.

Tokeen is located at the bottom of the funnel-shaped El Capitan Passage, which narrows northward for fifteen miles before making a sharp dogleg to the west. Though logging is heavy (particularly on the east shore), El Capitan Passage retains a lot of its charm, with light marine traffic through it and many still pristine spots. Watch for black bears along the shore.

Devilfish Bay is shrouded in myths that still affect visitors. Tlingit legends tell of a huge octopus (devilfish) that rose from the bay to destroy an entire village. Geologists who camped in Devilfish Bay a few years ago were so overcome by the malevolent mood of the place that they fled. Local people scoff: "They told each other too many ghost stories around the fire." (I admit to having hurried by along the opposite shore of El Capitan Passage.)

At Aneskett Point, the passage bends sharply to the west, passing a Forest Service camp and a logging haul road on the north shore. The mountains to the northwest are spectacular as seen from here. Particularly impressive is the granitic, barren Mount Calder, named by George Vancouver for a fellow naval officer in 1793.

The passage narrows to less than a hundred yards in Dry Pass. Once it was just that—a dry pass—on lower tides, but the Corps of Engineers dredged a seven-foot-deep channel to allow fishing boats and log rafts to use the pass. At low tide the area is reminiscent of a strip mine with dredged piles of gravel piled here and there. Nonetheless, it is an interesting passage with dozens of navigation markers to mark the channel through the expansive tide flats that surround portions of the route. The current can run at up to two knots through the pass, so aim to catch the ebb for a free ride.

Just beyond Dry Pass was the community of Shakan (pronounced Sha-*can*), an ancient Tlingit settlement which became a sawmill site in the late nineteenth century. But there is nothing to see there now. All traces of settlement were obliterated by recent logging.

The coast between Shakan Bay and Point Baker is exposed to the open water of Sumner Strait, with few places to shelter along the four-mile stretch between Barrier Island and Labouchere Bay. An exception is Hole in the Wall, a narrow cleft between the sea cliffs leading almost a mile to a placid lagoon where fishing boats have long found refuge from the strait's weather. Level grassy areas surround the anchorage amid high, rocky peaks—well worth a look.

Civilization begins again at Labouchere Bay, where there are a logging camp and Forest Service work center connected to the network of haul roads on Prince of Wales Island. The communities of Port Protection and Point Baker just to the north successfully resisted construction of a road to their towns, preferring a life-style dominated by boats and excluding cars. A good part of Point Baker floats instead of resting on land. You will see floating houses, fish-buying stations, and the Trading Post (which is also a café and one of the few floating bars in Alaska). This is the local center for trolling and gill-netting fleets that fish the Sumner Strait area.

The paddle east across the northern end of Prince of Wales follows clearcut shores, where bands of timber have been left near the mouths of streams in the many coves along the way. Red Bay, once noted for its exceptional beauty, still holds charm in spite of logging scars and has an active history of canneries and salteries.

Consider the weather carefully before undertaking the three-and-a-halfmile crossing to Zarembo Island. Snow Passage can become very rough in a southerly wind. Zarembo Island looks much like north Prince of Wales—logged right down to the beach, though stream-side exceptions still afford campsites. The coastal waters north toward St. John's harbor are shallow, and choppy in wind. The fishing is poor, although commercial crabbers are successful there. The logging camp at St. John's Harbor has been dismantled, with only caretakers present when I passed through in 1982. The harbor is known for its carbonated-water springs. That water was being bottled and shipped to Seattle early in this century. Uncovered only at low tide, the springs make the inner harbor waters bubble gently when the tide is in. The camp has a connection to the spring; ask the caretaker about it.

North of St. John's, you have the option of continuing east to Wrangell or crossing north to Mitkof Island and following the Wrangell Narrows to Petersburg (about the same distance as to Wrangell), a trip previously described.

The Central British Columbia Coast, Southward from Ocean Falls

OVERVIEW: This is the country that marks the beginning of the wild North Coast above Vancouver Island. There is no road access within this region, and the waterways are its highways. The route described includes travel in narrow, fjordlike channels along the Inside Passage and in the open ocean of Queen Charlotte Sound. Depending on the options taken, trips can be as short as a thirty-mile paddle between Ocean Falls and Bella Bella, or a two-hundred-mile, three-week expedition from Ocean Falls to Port Hardy. Though the long version is only for skilled and adventuresome kayakers with open-ocean experience, sources of supply and emergency assistance seldom are far away, with four manned lighthouses, fish-buying scows, and settlements scattered along the way.

ACCESS: Highway 19 to Port Hardy (north Vancouver Island); British Columbia ferry to Ocean Falls; optional return to Port Hardy by B.C. ferry from Bella Bella, or optional scheduled flights (Air B.C.) to Bella Bella or Namu from either Port Hardy or Vancouver.

Fisher Channel

The Central British Columbia Coast

(not for navigation purposes)

SUPPLY POINTS: Port Hardy, Ocean Falls, Bella Bella, Namu, fish-buying scows probable in Finn Bay (north of Rivers Inlet).

CHARTS AND OTHER NAVIGATION AIDS: Canadian nautical chart 3270 for the short trip to Bella Bella. Continuation to Port Hardy requires charts 3785, 3784, 3727, 3779, 3776, 3551, and 3574. Use *Canadian Tide and Current Tables,* Volume 6.

On the extended trip to Port Hardy, folding-boat owners have the option of shortening the trip by taking Air B.C.'s scheduled service from Namu to Port Hardy. (This and flights to Vancouver have been on-again-off-again in the recent past, so check before you start your trip.) There also is the option of avoiding the last and most challenging third of the trip by arranging for a plane chartered from Air B.C., in Port Hardy, to pick you up in Rivers Inlet or Smith Sound. Rigid kayaks could be transported either inside or strapped to the pontoons of the Otter aircraft. Make preliminary plans with the charter firm before you depart and then confirm your pickup by telephone at Namu, by radio-telephone at the Finn Bay fish-buying scow, or at Duncanby Landing, a fishing-boat servicing station just south of Rivers Inlet.

Allow three weeks for the Ocean Falls—Port Hardy trip (assuming an average daily distance of ten miles). Since paddling in Queen Charlotte Sound and Strait is dependent on good weather, try to get ahead of schedule on the first half of the trip, thereby allowing plenty of time to await good traveling conditions on the exposed portions. You probably will want to spend more time in that area anyway, because of its outer-coast environment.

Both routes begin at Ocean Falls, once the second-largest town on the central B.C. coast. Though the schedule changes from year to year, the B.C. ferry generally stops at Ocean Falls once a week, northbound from Port Hardy or southbound from Prince Rupert.

Until 1980, Ocean Falls was a community of fifteen hundred people. In that year, the pulp mill that was the basis of its existence closed. Now, Ocean Falls is home for only seventy-five souls: a caretaker crew (for the mill, other buildings, and company-owned residences), some fishermen, and a few hand-loggers. The hospital, the small department store, the school, and Royal Canadian Mounted Police offices all are closed. However, there are services for the visitor—a hotel, a restaurant open during regular meal hours, and a small store with basic groceries and supplies.

The country around Ocean Falls is precipitously mountainous, with bare, rocky peaks all around. Some views from the inlet remind me of California's Yosemite Valley. The walk to the dam at the head of the falls next to the mill is well worth it, with views down the long, winding lake, which could be taken for yet another arm of the sea in this fjord country.

Begin paddling from Ocean Falls through Cousins Inlet to its junction with

Fisher Channel. The shores of both of these are steep, with few haul-out or campsite possibilities, so begin your trip early in the day and in good weather. The country flattens out in the vicinity of the mouth of Johnson Channel, where campsite prospects are much brighter. At this point, the route to Bella Bella branches to the west into Gunboat Passage.

Gunboat Passage to Bella Bella

Gunboat Passage is a narrow, twisting channel that is nonetheless occasionally used by large vessels. In August 1982, the B.C. ferry *Queen of Prince Rupert* ran aground in the passage, but was able to back off and return to Bella Bella. The ferry does not usually take this route and, reportedly, part of a group of local Indians boarding at Bella Bella got off again when they heard she was going through the passage. Others of the group stayed on, but took up a station on the bow. When they saw that the ship was indeed going to hit, they ran all the way to the stern and were standing by the lifeboats when the impact came. (Fortunately, the lifeboats were not needed.)

The passage was named for two gunboats, *Grappler* and *Forward,* that patrolled the region between 1860 and 1870. There are many coves on either side that invite exploration. Currents are fast through the passage, so travel with the ebb tide.

After exiting Gunboat Passage, follow the shore of Denny Island five miles to the community of Shearwater, well worth a visit. This was a patrol seaplane base during World War II and now has a restaurant and a cabaret that does a thriving business with fishermen and the residents of Bella Bella during the summer season. A mile or so west is a cold-storage plant operated by a native cooperative.

Old Bella Bella and New Bella Bella face each other across the mile-wide Lama Passage. Just to the south, the passage constricts to little more than a few hundred yards. This is one of the narrowest points on B.C.'s Inside Passage, forcing the Alaska and B.C. ferries and cruise ships to slow down and steer carefully, particularly because of the fishing boat traffic streaming in and out of Bella Bella.

Old Bella Bella, on the east shore, consists of only a few buildings, one of them a general store that carries a surprisingly complete line of supplies. New Bella Bella is the Indian community, known to the Bella Bella Band (members of the Central Kwakiutl grouping) as Waglisla. There you will find a restaurant, hotel, and community store. The B.C. ferry docks in New Bella Bella. The ferry takes on no cars at Bella Bella, so if you plan to board there, ask the ferry personnel how to get your kayak down to the car deck, from which you will exit at your destination.

There are countless opportunities for loop trips out of Bella Bella—northwest to Milbanke Sound, west to the Bardswell Group, or south to the labyrinth of islands around Queen Sound. These areas are predominantly rocky, with scrubby growth ashore. But intricate, kayak-size waterways and an occasional but superb beach make them well worth visiting. Trips west and south of Bella Bella are well described in Ince and Kottner's *Sea Kayaking Canada's West Coast* (see Appendix).

If you are continuing the journey south to Port Hardy via the Inside Passage, follow Lama Passage south and then east to its junction with Fisher Channel.

Ocean Falls or Bella Bella to Port Hardy

From Ocean Falls, the most direct route is south along Fisher Channel to Fitz Hugh Sound. Making the optional side trip to Bella Bella adds about twenty miles to the total distance.

After paddling south along Fisher Channel to the Johnson Channel junction (already described), you may wish to cross to the east shore at Salisbury Cone (a conspicuous peak), as this is one of the narrowest points and there are some interesting features along the eastern shore as you journey south. Codville Lagoon is intriguing to explore. The hills around the lagoon are largely bare rock and should make easy hiking and provide good vistas to the north and south.

As with other channels and inlets that must be crossed farther south, cross Burke Channel as close as possible to slack tide. The channel drains a huge network of waterways to the east and currents may be strong. Watch for rips and a heavy chop that may develop from an ebb tide flowing against a southerly wind.

Namu, a few miles south of Burke Channel, is a company town operated by B.C. Packers, which processes fish from the large troller and gill-net fleets in the area. Though there is no restaurant, meals can be purchased during limited hours at the mess hall. You will find a well-supplied store and a post office. There is a long history of Indian occupancy in Namu. Behind the mess hall, archeologists from Simon Fraser University have excavated a midden area, where they found a human skeleton at least six feet below the current ground level.

Continue along the east shore of Fitz Hugh Sound. The beaches at Koeye River and the abandoned lime kiln operation are worth your time, as is a paddle a mile inland to a scenic, open valley. This is grizzly bear country, so be careful.

To the south, the country becomes more broken, with a chain of islands that provide interesting paddling and protection from the weather. There is a manned lighthouse station on Addenbroke Island. Just north of Rivers Inlet is Finn Bay, on the north side of Penrose Island. In most years, a fish-buying scow which sells groceries anchors here during the fishing season. Take time to explore the maze of islands south and east of Penrose Island, where little, jewellike beaches may be found.

Rivers Inlet is a mecca for salmon, which are pursued by large numbers of both commercial and sport fishermen during July and August. There once were canneries in almost every cove along its shores, but all are now defunct. Many have been converted into sport-fishing resorts. There is one such resort on your route, at Goose Bay, but visitors other than paying guests reportedly are not welcome. Instead, head west to Cranstown Point, a beautiful spot with sandy beaches on either side of an isthmus.

Beyond Cranstown Point, you will enter the exposed coastline bordering Queen Charlotte Sound. Boaters of all kinds hesitate before they cross this body of water, open to the Pacific. For the most part, the coastline offers good protection for kayaks that can take advantage of the offshore rocks and use the many tiny coves for shelter. Nonetheless, treat this portion of your journey with respect. Look ahead on your chart before you venture forth each day, and be sure to keep haul-out opportunities in mind should the weather turn sour. There is a manned lighthouse on Egg Island west of Smith Sound, though the approach to it is across exposed seas.

The safest crossing of Smith Sound is a few miles inside it, where there are islands in the middle. On the south side of the sound is tiny Jones Cove, behind Macnicol Point. Small boats often wait there for good weather before they head south around Cape Caution to Queen Charlotte Strait. Camping is poor in the cove because of the brush, though there is more open country a hundred yards or so inland from the head of the cove.

You can find landings in all but strong northwesterly winds in the bays and coves between Smith Sound and Cape Caution, but this stretch of coastline should be navigated only in calm weather. The beaches in this area are exceptional.

You will be most at the mercy of the elements rounding Cape Caution and along the seven miles beyond to Slingsby Channel, as there are few safe landing places in rough weather. This is a good place for prudence; wait for good weather and get an early start in the morning. Finally, Slingsby Channel has very fast currents, as it drains the hundred-odd-mile-long Seymour Inlet through passages less than a quarter-mile wide. The ends of the channel are the worst. The outer narrows can run at nine knots; Nakwakto Rapids can attain sixteen knots! Stay to the west of Fox Island and then head in to shelter to its south. Beyond, the coastline is protected by offshore islands.

Your chart probably will show an abandoned town at Allison Harbour. I was unable to find any traces of it. As a consolation prize, the harbor and surrounding waters turned out to be interesting to explore.

At this point, you will need to consider crossing Queen Charlotte Strait to Port Hardy. Southeast squalls can make this a very dangerous body of water. I recommend a bit of a detour to use the islands to break up the crossing as much as possible. Continue along the mainland shore until opposite the Millar Group Islands. Look for the light operated by a small wind generator in the Jeannette Islands and then cross to the Millars. Be watchful for heavy marine traffic there, as this is the main Inside Passage route. The longest crossing will be from the Deserter Group to Bell Island, about three miles. Also be careful in Goletas Channel, where even in fair weather, westerlies funneling through it can be very strong.

APPENDICES

Equipment Checklist

Following is a list of equipment that is essential, useful, or simply "nice to have" in a kayak on the North Coast. The list is oriented toward longer trips (a week or more). For shorter ones, or if you are inclined to travel light, some items can be eliminated. I have noted these optional pieces of equipment with an asterisk.

BOAT ACCESSORIES

Paddle(s) and spare
Spray skirt(s) or spray cover
Life jacket(s)
Bilge pump
Sponge
Bowline (fifty feet or longer)
Flotation or dry-storage bags
Folding boat storage bags
Rescue system (stirrup or self-
    rescue outrigger components)
Sea anchor*
Sail or kite*

REPAIR KIT

Duct tape
Soft annealed wire (coil of five feet)
Small vise-grip pliers
Hacksaw blade (piece four inches
    long)
1/16-inch drill bit
WD-40 or similar lubricant*
Swiss Army knife or equivalent
Reinforced strapping tape*
Self-vulcanizing bicycle tube patches
    (for boot repair)*

For fiberglass boats: patching kit
    (cloth, mat, resin, and catalyst),
    50-grit sandpaper
For folding boats: hull patching kit
    (material and adhesive), heavy
    needle and thread, replacement
    fittings

NAVIGATIONAL EQUIPMENT

Nautical charts and chart case
Current and tide tables
Compass
Binoculars*
Weather radio*

EMERGENCY SIGNALING
    EQUIPMENT

Flares and smoke devices
EPIRB*
VHF or CB transmitter*

SURVIVAL EQUIPMENT

Wet suit or exposure suit*
Whistle
Waterproof matches and fire starter

High-energy food source
Tea or bouillon
Personal shelter—compact plastic or
    metalized body-size bag
Flare or smoke device
Container for survival kit—money
    belt, vest, or pockets in life jacket

First-Aid Kit

Seasickness pills
Pain-killer
Ace bandage
Gauze roll
Sterile compresses
Butterfly closures
Triangular bandage
Adhesive tape
Safety pins
Fast-acting emetic and laxative (if
    shellfish to be eaten)
Aspirin
Antibiotic pills*
Remedy for digestive upset
Burn ointment (anesthetic)
Antibacterial ointment
Tweezers
Scissors
First-aid book
Storage book (waterproof)

Clothing

Quick-drying pants (two pairs)
Wool pants*
Long underwear*
Wool socks (three pairs or more)
Changes of underwear
Polypropylene undershirt or
    turtleneck
Wool shirt
Sweater
Vest or jacket (synthetic fill)
Wool hat

Sou'wester rain hat
Foul-weather jacket and pants
Rubber gloves, Pogies, or other
    paddling gloves*
Footwear for wading: rubber boots,
    "Maine guide shoe" type, or wet
    suit bootees
Sneakers or other footgear for
    walking ashore

Personal Equipment

Sleeping bag (synthetic fill), stuff
    bag, and waterproof plastic bag
    (goes inside stuff bag)
Ground pad
Towel
Sunglasses
Tent
Tarp
Lighter and/or waterproof matches
Fire starter
Saw or hatchet*
Mosquito repellent
Toilet paper
Small flashlight
Candles
Toilet articles
Shower components*
Dry storage bags for clothing and
    other equipment
Duffel bags
Tote bag for loose items
Camera and storage bag
Defensive firearm (in brown bear
    country)*
Bear bell
Diving gear*
Fishing gear*

Cooking Equipment

Stove and fuel*
Cook set

Fry pan*
Eating utensils
Spatula*
Dish soap and scrubber
Cup
Spices
Food
Food storage bags (Ziploc)
Water container (two-gallon or
    larger)
Guide to edible plants*

Marine Weather
Broadcasting Stations

These are invaluable for making decisions about traveling, especially if you have a crossing to make or will be venturing onto the open Pacific. All are VHF frequencies, and can be received on radios with a weather band, "weather cube" radios, or a VHF set. The range of each station is rarely more than forty miles, and less if there are intervening hills (climbing a hill with your radio may make a big difference).

ALASKA (NOAA STATIONS)	FREQUENCY
Anchorage	A
Cordova	A
Homer	B
Juneau	A
Ketchikan	A
Kodiak	A
Petersburg	A
Seward	A
Sitka	B
Valdez	A
Wrangell	B
Yakutat	A

British Columbia (Coast Guard stations)	Frequency
Alert Bay	A
Holberg peripheral	C
Comox	A
Prince Rupert	C
Sandspit, B.C. (reports at 0110, 0440, 0935, 1050, 1420, 1840, 1920, 2120 hours)	C
Tofino	C
Eliza Dome peripheral (Nootka Sound)	C
Vancouver	C
Victoria	C

Frequencies:

A	162.55 MegaHertz
B	162.40 MegaHertz
C	161.65 MegaHertz

Useful Addresses

KAYAKS

Included here is a variety of sea kayak manufacturers and selected retailers that carry either a wide range of kayaks or ones not commonly available from other outlets.

Easy Rider Canoe and Kayak Co.
P.O. Box 88108
Tukwila Branch
Seattle, WA 98188
(206) 228-3633
(kayaks and accessories)

Ecomarine Ocean Kayak Center
1668 Duranleau Street
Vancouver, B.C. V6H 3S4
(604) 689-7575
(wide variety of folding and rigid
   kayaks)

Eddyline Kayak Works
P.O. Box 842
Paine Field South Complex
Building 302
Everett, WA 98204
(206) 743-9252
(kayaks and accessories)

Folbot Corporation
BP 282
Charleston, SC 29405-0877
(803) 744-3483
(folding kayaks; send $1 for catalog)

Werner A. Furrer
Northwest Design Works

3512 N.E. 92nd
Seattle, WA 98115
(206) 524-9749
(Seagull kayak and fiberglass
   paddles)

Hans Klepper Corporation
35 Union Square West
New York, NY 10003
(212) 243-3428
(folding kayaks)

Mariner Kayaks
1005 East Spruce
Seattle, WA 98122
(206) 322-1658 or 622-7215
(kayaks and accessories)

Pacific Canoe Base
2155 Dowler Place
Victoria, B.C. V8T 4H2
(604) 382-1243
(specializing in British-style kayaks:
   Nordkapp, Umnak, Icefloe,
   Baiderka)

Pacific Water Sports
16205 Pacific Highway South
Seattle, WA 98188
(206) 246-9385

CHARTS AND NAVIGATIONAL REFERENCES

Captain's Nautical Supplies
Fishermen's Terminal
Seattle, WA 98119
(206) 283-7242
(Alaska and B.C. charts and navigation aids)

Canadian Hydrographic Service
P.O. Box 6000
Sidney, B.C. V8L 4B2
(604) 656-8358
(British Columbia charts)

Distribution Division (OA/C44)
National Ocean Survey
Riverside, MD 20840
(301) 436-6990
(NOAA charts of Alaska)

TRANSPORTATION

Air B.C.
4680 Cowley Crescent
Richmond, B.C. V7B 1C1
(800) 663-9545

Air B.C.
Airport Road
Port Hardy, B.C. V0N 2P0
(604) 949-6353

Alberni Marine Transportation Co.
P.O. Box 118
Port Alberni, B.C. V9Y 7M7
(604) 723-9774
(M/V *Lady Rose*)

Alaska Exploration Holidays
1500 Metropolitan Park Building
Seattle, WA 98101

(800) 426-0600 (from outside Washington)
(206) 624-8551 (from within Washington)
(M/V *Thunder Bay* and Glacier Bay Lodge reservations)

Alaska Marine Highway Systems
Pouch R
Juneau, AK 99811
(907) 465-3941 (Juneau)
(206) 623-1970 (Seattle terminal)

British Columbia Ferry Corporation
818 Broughton Street
Victoria, B.C. V8W 1E4
(604) 669-1211 (Vancouver)
(604) 386-3431 (Victoria)

British Columbia Steamship Company, Ltd.
254 Belleville Street
Victoria, B.C. V8V 1W9
(604) 386-6731 (Victoria)
(206) 683-5560 (Seattle)

Channel Flying, Inc.
2601 Channel Drive
Juneau, AK 99801
(907) 586-3331

Glacier Bay Yacht/Seaplane Tours
P.O. Box 424
Juneau, AK 99802
(907) 586-6835

Nootka Sound Service, Ltd.
P.O. Box 28
Port Alberni, B.C. V9Y 7M6
(604) 723-3132
(M/V *Uchuck III*)

Southeast Alaska Airlines
1515 Tongass Avenue
Ketchikan, AK 99901
(907) 225-6691
(Scheduled and chartered flights)

Trans Provincial Airlines, Ltd.
P.O. Box 280
Prince Rupert, B.C. V8J 3P6
(604) 627-1341

Trans Provincial Airlines, Ltd.
P.O. Box 224
Sandspit, B.C. V0T 1T0
(604) 637-5355

Ward Air
1873 Shell Simmons Drive, Suite
   5118
Juneau, AK 99801
(907) 789-9150

GOVERNMENT AGENCIES AND LOCAL ADMINISTRATIONS

Glacier Bay National Park and
   Preserve
Gustavus, AK 99826
(907) 698-3341

Department of Fisheries and Oceans
1090 West Pender Street
Vancouver, B.C. V6E 2P1
(604) 666-1384
(information on fishing licenses in
   British Columbia)

Ministry of Lands, Parks, and
   Housing
1019 Wharf Street
Victoria, B.C. V8W 2Y9
(information on Ecological Reserves:

Lands Branch; on Permits for
   Provincial Parks: Parks Branch)

Pacific Rim National Park
P.O. Box 280
Ucluelet, B.C. V0R 3A0

Skidegate Band of the Haida
Rural Route 1, Box 1
Queen Charlotte City, B.C. V0T 1S0
(604) 559-4496

United States Forest Service
Tongass National Forest
Chatham Area
P.O. Box 1980
Sitka, AK 99835

United States Forest Service
Tongass National Forest
Ketchikan Area
Federal Building
Ketchikan, AK 99901

United States Forest Service
Tongass National Forest
Stikine Area
Box 309
Petersburg, AK 99833

KAYAK RENTALS IN GLACIER BAY

Alaska Discovery
Glacier Bay Office
P.O. Box 26
Gustavus, AK 99826
(907) 697-3431
(kayak rentals and guided trips)

Related Reading

Alaska Shipper's Guide. Anchorage: Alaska Northwest Publishing Company, 1983 Edition.
   This annual publication is a useful resource if you are considering shipping your kayak to remote places by barge or air freight.

Boehm, William D. *Glacier Bay: Old Ice, New Land*. Alaska Geographic Vol.3, No.1 (1975).
   A fine photo essay of an other-worldly place, its physiography, flora, and fauna. The book includes hiking directions for highlands adjoining the upper reaches of the bay.

Bultmann, Phyllis, and Bultmann, Bill. *Border Boating: Twelve Cruises through the San Juan and Gulf Islands*. Seattle: Pacific Search Press, 1979.
   Here are good details on things to see and places to stop in the islands when traveling by kayak or in any other boat.

Carey, Neil B. *A Guide to the Queen Charlotte Islands*. 6th ed. Anchorage: Alaska Northwest Publishing Company, 1982.
   A detailed tour of the Charlottes' fascinating places and their rich histories. The author is a long-time resident of the islands.

Craven, Margaret. *I Heard the Owl Call My Name*. New York: Dell Publishing Company, 1974.
   A lyrical novel of present-day Indian life in a backwater inlet east of Queen Charlotte Strait. As a result of the flood of attention this book has drawn to Kingcove Inlet, visitors are no longer entirely welcome there. Absorb the beauty of this book...and go elsewhere.

Dolan, Jonni. *Two Crows Came*. Seattle: Pacific Search Press, 1980.
   A true tale of a Puget Sound family gill-net fishing in Southeast Alaska. Provides fine insights about the varying outlooks and nonconformities found in the community of commercial fishermen.

Dowd, John. *Sea Kayaking: A Manual for Long-Distance Touring*. 2d ed. rev. Vancouver: Douglas and McIntyre, and Seattle: University of Washington

Press, 1983.
Already the classic of sea kayaking, Dowd's book is the best available for ocean voyaging worldwide. In the revised edition, Dowd balances his preference for folding boats with a good buyer's analysis of rigid kayaks, largely a product of his recent experience as proprietor of Ecomarine Ocean Kayak Center in Vancouver.

Eppenbach, Sarah. *Alaska's Southeast: Touring the Inside Passage*. Seattle: Pacific Search Press, 1983.
Those interested in visiting the towns and more remote villages of the Inside Passage will find this the best overall guide available. Chapters on Southeast's history, native heritage, wildlife, and plants flesh out the description of what there is to see and do in each town. Also included is a section on wilderness lodges accessible only by air or water.

Furrer, Werner. *Water Trails of Washington*. Rev. ed. Edmonds, WA: Signpost Books, 1979.
Though this book concentrates on rivers in western Washington, it includes a few short saltwater trips in the Puget Sound area. The author is one of the Northwest's veteran sea kayakers.

Hilson, Stephen E. *Exploring Alaska and British Columbia: Skagway to Barkley Sound*. Holland, MI: Van Winkle Publishing, 1976.
A most useful volume for trip planning, with annotated charts of the entire coast and inland waterways between Vancouver Island (including its west coast) and Skagway, Alaska. Though the charts are a bit small for navigation, they include a wealth of useful historical information and notations about available services in outlying communities.

Hutchinson, Derek. *Sea Canoeing*. Rev. ed. London: Adam and Charles Black, Ltd., 1979.
This was the first book on modern sea kayaking. It reflects the British approach—athletes paddling narrow boats. Good information about paddle-work in tough situations, including heavy weather and surf.

Ince, John, and Kottner, Hedi. *Sea Kayaking Canada's West Coast*. Vancouver: Raxas Press, 1982.
This guidebook covers the entire west coast of Vancouver Island from Barkley Sound to Cape Scott, most of the island waterways to the east of the island, and includes a few trips north of there. The descriptions are enriched by sensitive treatments of each area's history and the life-styles of current residents.

Johannsen, Neil, and Johannsen, Betty. *Exploring Alaska's Prince William*

Sound. Anchorage: Alaska Travel Publications, 1975.
If you are going there, this is the book to have, with place-specific details and fine treatment of the natural and human history of the area.

L'Amour, Louis. *Sitka.* New York: Bantam Books, 1981.
This novel tells a swashbuckling tale of nineteenth-century Russian Alaska. Particularly of interest to kayakers is the episode at Tenakee Portage. Is it believable? Make the portage and decide for yourself.

Marine Sciences Directorate, Department of the Environment.
Sailing Directions, British Columbia Coast (North Portion) Cape Caution to Portland Inlet, including the south coast of Alaska and the Queen Charlotte Islands, Vol. II, 8th ed., 1980.

McGary, Noel, and Lincoln, John W. *Tide Prints: Surface Tidal Currents in Puget Sound.* Seattle: University of Washington Press, 1977.
This is a useful graphic tool for interpreting current patterns in Puget Sound as they change through the tidal cycle. Unfortunately, the complex and problematic currents of the San Juan Islands are not included.

The Milepost. Anchorage: Alaska Northwest Publishing Company, 1983 edition.
An excellent resource for trip planning in Alaska, including Southeast and the B.C. coast. Good information on highways, water transportation, and local communities.

Piggott, Margaret. *Discover Southeast Alaska with Pack and Paddle.* Seattle: The Mountaineers, 1978.
Though the emphasis is on hiking, this guidebook includes extensive information on paddling in Glacier Bay and on the coast of West Chichagof Island. Some of the information on transporation is badly out of date.

Roppel, Patricia. *Southeast: Alaska's Panhandle.* Alaska Geographic Vol. 5, No. 2 (1978).
This book is the best way to get to know the region. It includes photos and a short vignette of almost every town and hamlet in Southeast.

Szczawinski, Adam F., and Hardy, George A. *Guide to Common Edible Plants of British Columbia.* Handbook No. 20. 4th ed. Victoria: British Columbia Provincial Museum, 1972.
This is the book from which I learned; it goes along whenever I head north. Most of the plants included also are found in Southeast Alaska.

Upton, Joe. *Alaska Blues: A Fisherman's Journal.* Anchorage: Alaska Northwest Publishing Company, 1977.

This award-winning journal is a sensitive monument to the independent Alaska commercial fisherman and his contest with capricious fish runs, regulatory agencies, and luck.

U.S. Coast Pilots and British Columbia Sailing Directories.
These provide good information for kayakers regarding local weather and sea conditions, some natural features ashore, services available in communities, and even the locations of some fish-buying scows.

U.S. Department of Commerce, National Oceanic and Atmospheric Administration. *United States Coast Pilot* Vol. 8, Pacific Coast Alaska: Dixon Entrance to Cape Spencer. Washington, 1980.

Index

Boldface numerals indicate pages on which photographs, illustrations, tables, or maps appear.

Personal Log

Other Books from Pacific Search Press

Alaska's Southeast: Touring the Inside Passage by Sarah Eppenbach
The Apple Cookbook by Kyle D. Fulwiler
Asparagus: The Sparrowgrass Cookbook by Autumn Stanley
The Bean Cookbook: Dry Legume Cookery by Norma S. Upson
The Berry Cookbook by Kyle D. Fulwiler
The Birdhouse Book: Building Houses, Feeders, and Baths by Don McNeil
Bone Appétit! Natural Foods for Pets by Frances Sheridan Goulart
Border Boating: Twelve Cruises through the San Juan and Gulf Islands by
    Phyllis and Bill Bultmann
Butterflies Afield in the Pacific Northwest by William Neill/Douglas Hepburn,
    photography
Canning and Preserving without Sugar by Norma M. MacRae, R.D.
The Carrot Cookbook by Ann Saling
Cascade Companion by Susan Schwartz/Bob and Ira Spring, photography
The Chilkat Dancing Blanket by Cheryl Samuel
Common Seaweeds of the Pacific Coast by J. Robert Waaland
The Complete Guide to Organic Gardening West of the Cascades by Steve
    Solomon
The Crawfish Cookbook by Norma S. Upson
Cross-Country Downhill and Other Nordic Mountain Skiing Techniques (2d
    Ed. Revised & Enlarged) by Steve Barnett
*Cruising the Columbia and Snake Rivers: Eleven Cruises in the Inland Water-
    way* by Sharlene P. Nelson and Joan LeMieux
The Dogfish Cookbook by Russ Mohney
The Eggplant Cookbook by Norma S. Upson
Fire and Ice: The Cascade Volcanoes (Revised Ed.) by Stephen L. Harris
A Fish Feast by Charlotte Wright
Food 101: A Student Guide to Quick and Easy Cooking by Cathy Smith
The Getaway Guide I: Short Vacations in the Pacific Northwest (2d Ed. Revised
    & Enlarged) by Marni and Jake Rankin
The Getaway Guide II: More Short Vacations in the Pacific Northwest by Marni
    and Jake Rankin
The Getaway Guide III: Short Vacations in Northern California by Marni and
    Jake Rankin
The Getaway Guide IV: Short Vacations in Southern California by Marni and
    Jake Rankin

The Green Tomato Cookbook by Paula Simmons

The Guide to Successful Tapestry Weaving by Nancy Harvey

The Handspinner's Guide to Selling by Paula Simmons

The House Next Door: Seattle's Neighborhood Architecture by Lila Gault/Mary Randlett, photography

Journey to the High Southwest: A Traveler's Guide by Robert L. Casey

Little Mammals of the Pacific Northwest by Ellen B. Kritzman

Living Shores of the Pacific Northwest by Lynwood Smith/Bernard Nist, photography

Make It and Take It: Homemade Gear for Camp and Trail by Russ Mohney

Marine Mammals of Eastern North Pacific and Arctic Waters edited by Delphine Haley

Messages from the Shore by Victor B. Scheffer

Minnie Rose Lovgreen's Recipe for Raising Chickens by Minnie Rose Lovgreen

Mushrooms 'n Bean Sprouts: A First Step for Would-be Vegetarian by Norma M. MacRae, R.D.

My Secret Cookbook by Paula Simmons

The Natural Fast Food Cookbook by Gail L. Worstman

The Natural Fruit Cookbook by Gail L. Worstman

One Potato, Two Potato: A Cookbook by Constance Bollen and Marlene Blessing

The Pike Place Market: People, Politics, and Produce by Alice Shorett and Murray Morgan

Rhubarb Renaissance: A Cookbook by Ann Saling

The River Pioneers: Early Days on Grays Harbor by Edwin Van Syckle

Roots & Tubers: A Vegetable Cookbook by Kyle D. Fulwiler

The Salmon Cookbook by Jerry Dennon

Seattle Photography by David Barnes

Sleek & Savage: North America's Weasel Family by Delphine Haley

Spinning and Weaving with Wool by Paula Simmons

Starchild & Holahan's Seafood Cookbook by Adam Starchild and James Holahan

They Tried to Cut It All by Edwin Van Syckle

Two Crows Came by Jonni Dolan

Warm & Tasty: The Wood Heat Stove Cookbook by Margaret Byrd Adams

The White-Water River Book: A Guide to Techniques, Equipment, Camping, and Safety by Ron Watters/Robert Winslow, photography

The Whole Grain Bake Book by Gail L. Worstman

Wild Mushroom Recipes by Puget Sound Mycological Society

Wild Shrubs: Finding and Growing Your Own by Joy Spurr

The Zucchini Cookbook (3d Ed. Revised & Enlarged) by Paula Simmons